MW01089468

COOKING & THE
CROWN

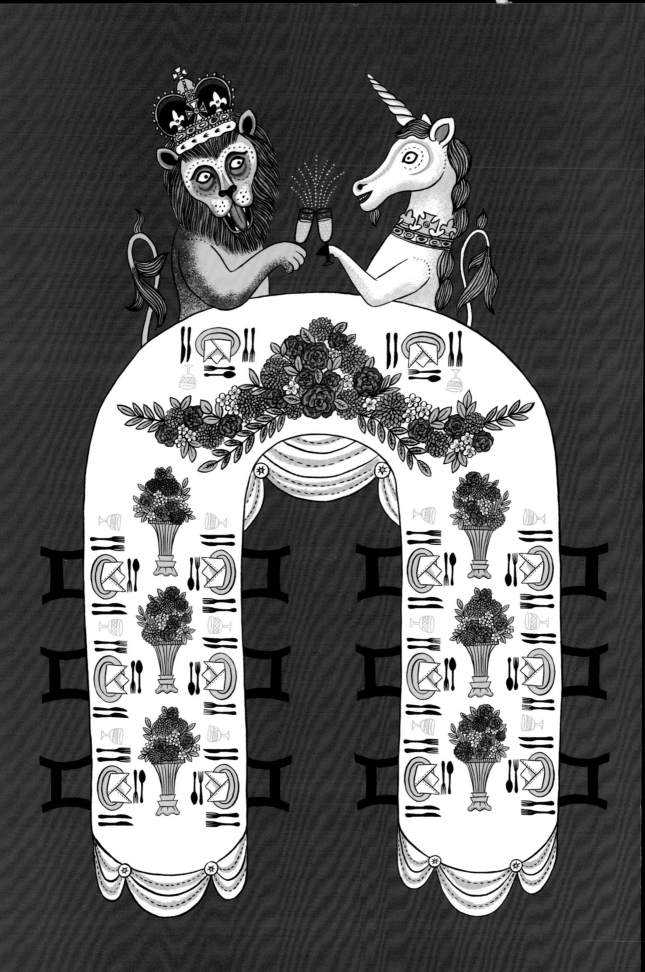

TOM
PARKER BOWLES
COOKING
& THE CROWN

Royal Recipes from
Queen Victoria to King Charles III

PHOTOGRAPHY BY JOHN CAREY
ILLUSTRATIONS BY ALICE PATTULLO

TEN SPEED PRESS
California | New York

Contents

In memory of
Queen Elizabeth II

*

For King Charles III
and Queen Camilla

Introduction

British royal food. For so long, the gilded pinnacle of gastronomy, a heady, regal extravaganza of excess where course after exquisite course emerged from cavernous kitchens—borne aloft by liveried footmen on plates of pure gold—to sate the whims of the richest, most powerful people on earth. For these banquets were no mere dinner, rather soufflé diplomacy at its most subtle, as kings, queens, and emperors, presidents, princes, and prime ministers quietly shaped history over *Mousses de Merlan à la Dieppoise* and *Cailles Rôties sur Canapé*.

And it was here, at these glittering, candlelit feasts in ancient castles and grand palaces alike, that the great chefs of the age—Carême, Francatelli, and the rest—were given the freedom (and budget) to create some of the most ornate, extravagant, and complex dishes ever seen. The original haute cuisine, and the standard to which all other chefs aspired, this was cooking as both art and inspiration, an entente cordiale of British ingredients and French technique.

These days, though, few of us have the time, skill, or inclination to debone a snipe, stuff a boar's head, or roast a whole haunch of ox. Nor spend three days preparing *Consommé au Faisan avec Quenelles*. Of course, back in the days of Queen Victoria and Edward VII, with a permanent kitchen staff of forty-five, anything was possible and everything expected. But as the years passed, brigades grew smaller, and lunches and dinners less, well, exhausting. Now, the King and Queen are positively abstemious. And although state banquets are still as important as ever, a direct link to the gilded gastronomic heights of the good old days, they never go on for more than three courses, plus coffee, fresh fruit, and petits fours.

This book, first and foremost, will be a tome for everyday use. I've spent months combing through archives, letters, diaries, cookbooks, and biographies to glean recipes that appeal to the modern cook. And don't require an entire kitchen brigade. Contrary to popular legend, it wasn't all lark's tongues and roast cygnet—although the latter was an occasional Christmas dish. No, the royal family, from Victoria onwards, have tastes like everyone else. Victoria was a devotee of cake, fruit, and all things sweet. Edward VII loved roast beef and Irish stew, George V liked curry, and mashed potatoes with everything, while his son, George VI, preferred his omelettes plain and unencumbered.

Of course, there are more recipes from the reigns of Queen Victoria and her son, Edward VII, as both were hearty eaters and ruled at a time when lavishly rich ten-course lunches and twelve-course dinners were par for the course. George V, in contrast to his father, had relatively simple tastes, although his wife, Queen Mary, was, in the words of royal chef Gabriel Tschumi, one of the "last great connoisseurs of food in England." Their son, George VI, was also a man who liked things straight and unadorned. And Queen Elizabeth II, while deeply knowledgeable about menus, special dishes, and state banquets (she never forgot a favorite dish eaten by any guest), had tastes that were many miles removed from extravagant.

As for King Charles III, I could write a whole different book on his knowledge of, and support for, British food and farming. In fact, there is no one better informed on everything from rare breeds and heritage fruit and vegetables to cheesemaking, butchery, and brewing. He is a genuine British food hero.

But if food is a prism through which one can see history and economics, then the cooking of the royal family offers a fascinating glimpse into the lives and habits of British society's upper strata. From the grand, if admittedly dyspeptic, excess of the Victorian and Edwardian ages, when cream, butter, foie gras, and truffles were used with giddy abandon, to wartime parsimony (no booze, and a mere two courses at breakfast!) and on into the modern world. Recipes are predominantly British and French (as French cooking was long seen as superior, at least in court circles), with occasional forays into India, Germany, and Italy. Not just a snapshot of the cooking of kings and queens, but a peek behind the scenes, an insight into royal kitchens, banquets, picnics, and barbecues. A taste of royal life.

Most of all, though, this is a book about pleasure, the joys of cooking and eating, of sitting down together and breaking bread. It's a celebration of the seasons, of great British ingredients, and a few French ones, too. You may be surprised at the simplicity of many of the recipes. That's the point. Food is the great leveler. I want to strip away the pomp and circumstance and get right to the meat of the matter—a collection of wonderful recipes that you really want to cook from over two centuries of regal eating.

Eat, drink, and be merry. Oh, and God Save the King and Queen!

Tom Parker Bowles

Coat of Arms

This is the Royal Coat of Arms of the United Kingdom, although a different version is used in Scotland. The lion (representing England) and unicorn (representing Scotland) are "supporters." They're "rampant" (or "rearing up") but the tongues are merely decorative. There are four quarters on the Shield: two are the three lions of England (gold on red), then a red lion for Scotland and a harp for Northern Ireland. The whole arms are surrounded by the Garter, inscribed with the motto of The Order of the Garter, *honi soit qui mal y pense*. Or "Shamed be whoever thinks ill of it."

Royal Family Tree

This is a hugely simplified royal family tree, concentrating, as this book does, on the British sovereigns, along with their husbands or wives. Because it would take page upon page to list the descendants of Victoria and Albert's nine children. Let alone the rest. Indeed, at one point, it seemed that most of Europe's royal families were related to Victoria. But as mother-in-law to the German Emperor and grandmother to Tsar Nicholas II, it's easy to see how she earned her nickname as "The Grandmother of Europe."

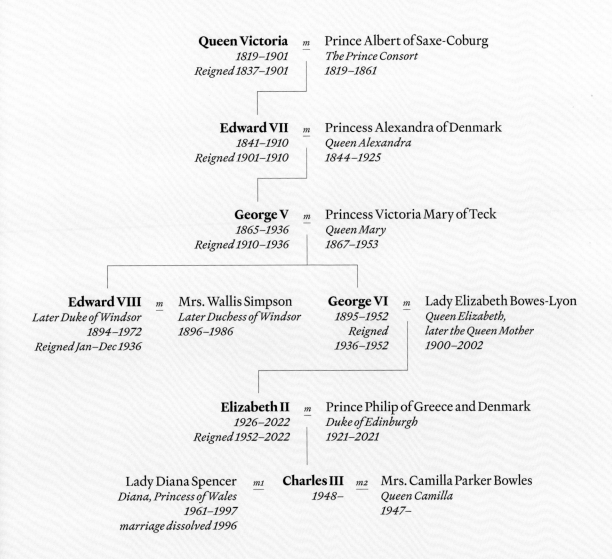

Queen Victoria   *m*   Prince Albert of Saxe-Coburg
1819–1901   *The Prince Consort*
Reigned 1837–1901   *1819–1861*

Edward VII   *m*   Princess Alexandra of Denmark
1841–1910   *Queen Alexandra*
Reigned 1901–1910   *1844–1925*

George V   *m*   Princess Victoria Mary of Teck
1865–1936   *Queen Mary*
Reigned 1910–1936   *1867–1953*

Edward VIII   *m*   Mrs. Wallis Simpson   **George VI**   *m*   Lady Elizabeth Bowes-Lyon
Later Duke of Windsor   *Later Duchess of Windsor*   *1895–1952*   *Queen Elizabeth,*
1894–1972   *1896–1986*   *Reigned*   *later the Queen Mother*
Reigned Jan–Dec 1936   *1936–1952*   *1900–2002*

Elizabeth II   *m*   Prince Philip of Greece and Denmark
1926–2022   *Duke of Edinburgh*
Reigned 1952–2022   *1921–2021*

Lady Diana Spencer   *m1*   **Charles III**   *m2*   Mrs. Camilla Parker Bowles
Diana, Princess of Wales   *1948–*   *Queen Camilla*
1961–1997   *1947–*
marriage dissolved 1996

Breakfast

Breakfast

"To eat well in England," the writer W. Somerset Maugham once joked, "you should have breakfast three times a day." He may have had a point. Because the aristocratic breakfasts of Victorian and Edwardian times were not so much dainty repasts as full-on gastronomic assaults, gut-busting epics that set one up for a good old-fashioned day's hunting, shooting, and roistering. Or simply getting on with ruling one's realm.

Breakfast was served in silver chafing dishes warmed with flickering spirit lamps. And this was the one meal where guests were expected to serve themselves. Well, with the obvious exception of sovereigns. Harold Nicolson, the upper-class polymath, described a typical upper-class spread of "hams, tongues, galantines, cold grouse, ditto partridge, ditto ptarmigan . . . the porridge would be disposed of negligently . . . then would come the whiting, and omelette, and devilled kidneys and little fishy messes in shells. And then scones and marmalade. And then a little melon, and a nectarine, and just one or two of those delicious raspberries." Breakfasts were, he noted wryly, "in no sense a hurried proceeding." Okay, so life back then was rather less sedentary, and a lack of central heating meant extra calories helped keep one warm. Still, it would take a hearty appetite to do such a feast justice. An appetite shared, fortuitously, by Queen Victoria and her son, Edward VII.

"I remember my surprise on coming down to the kitchens on the first day of my duties," writes Gabriel Tschumi in his memoir, *Royal Chef,* "to find that breakfast was as big a meal as the main meal of the day in Switzerland." He started as an apprentice in the Buckingham Palace kitchen in April 1898 before going on to cook under Edward VII and George V, eventually ending up as royal chef to Queen Mary. Seeing that lunch and dinner were usually ten courses long, he expected that "breakfast would be a very light meal indeed." How wrong he was. "I found, instead, that the coal ranges were red-hot and the spits packed with chops, cutlets, steaks, bloaters [whole smoked herring], sausages, chicken and woodcock. The roast chefs were deftly removing them and piling them onto huge platters. In other parts of the kitchen cooks were trimming rashers of streaky bacon, a quarter of an inch thick for grilling, and preparing egg dishes." The royal family would expect at least five dishes, as did the ladies- and gentlemen-in-waiting, who ate separately. "Any servant could have the same number of courses for breakfast," he noted. "Quite a number managed it daily without any trouble."

Queen Victoria enjoyed eating her breakfast *en plein air* in a tent on the lawn at Frogmore, in Windsor, and at Balmoral. Usually accompanied by the wheeze of bagpipes played by her personal piper—a tradition that goes on to this day. As was typical of contemporary accounts pertaining to the Queen, she was portrayed as having a suitably dainty appetite. "The Queen's breakfasts are even plainer than her luncheons," says the anonymous author, thought to be a high-ranking courtier, of *The Private Life of the Queen*. "Fish is always on the table, but eggs on toast, or merely boiled, with dry toast and a small selection of fancy toast, are the usual articles put before the Queen at her first meal." The author also notes that "the eggs served at the Queen's breakfast table are exclusively those of white Dorkings," from her flock at Windsor.

On her first visit to Scotland in autumn of 1842, "Her Majesty took oatmeal porridge at breakfast, tried the 'Finnan haddies,' and pronounced the homely Scottish fare excellent." Despite the popular myth, there's no evidence of breakfast curries, although after she was crowned Empress of India two Indian retainers were always at her side.

Victoria's son, Edward VII, was a magnificent eater, one of history's great trenchermen. As Sidney Lee, one of his many biographers, pointed out with admirable understatement, the King "never toyed with his food." Yet at breakfast, he was unusually restrained. "The King was no breakfast eater," wrote Sir Frederick "Fritz" Ponsonby, his equerry and assistant private secretary, "having only a cup of coffee and a bit of toast." The exception was made on shooting and racing days. Then, he'd devour small fried soles, bacon, eggs (either poached or *en cocotte*, a great favorite of his wife, Alexandra, who was as slim as her husband was broad), haddock *à l'anglaise,* deviled roast chicken, and a couple of *becassines sur canapés*, or roast woodcock on toast.

Edward's son, George V, was a markedly different character from his epicurean father. A staunch naval man, he'd have been content to survive on military rations and was dependably "regular" in his habits. Five days a week he ate eggs, crisp streaky bacon, and fish, either trout, plaice, or sole. On Saturdays, sausages, too "basted and well-grilled." The only time he strayed from this routine was when Yarmouth bloaters were in season. These replaced the bangers. His son, George VI, shared his father's restraint. And the variety of food was not much helped by Second World War rationing, which only ended in 1954, two years after his death.

Times change, along with appetites, although eggs still starred in the breakfasts of Queen Elizabeth II. Alongside orange juice, cereal, and toast. When the royal family gathered at Balmoral or Windsor, there might be kedgeree, *oeufs en cocotte*, Benedict, or Florentine. The King's breakfast is simply dried fruit and honey. Queen Camilla has yogurt in summer and porridge in winter. A thoroughly modern, and healthy, start to the day. But I'm not sure Victoria would have approved.

Queen Camilla's Porridge

In winter, my mother, Queen Camilla, eats porridge every day—plain, aside from a little of her own honey. The hives sit at the back of a field at Raymill, the house in which my sister and I spent the latter part of our youth. During winter, all is quiet. But come the summer, we tend to give those hives a wide berth. My mother gives most of her honey to Fortnum & Mason, where it is sold in special jars, with all proceeds going to one of her charities. It's delicate and mild, as fine stirred into a good Darjeeling tea as it is mixed with porridge or yogurt.

— Serves 1 —

½ cup/50g Scottish oatmeal or old-fashioned rolled oats

1½ cups/360ml whole milk

Pinch of salt

1 tsp honey

Put the oatmeal in a saucepan, add the milk and salt, and bring to a boil, then decrease the heat and simmer for about 5 minutes, until thick and creamy.

Add the honey and serve.

Baked Eggs

Baked eggs, also known as *oeufs en cocotte*, have long been a staple of the royal table, from Queen Victoria to the present day. The Duke of Windsor was a particular fan. This was also a favorite dish from my childhood, usually devoured when we returned home from our holidays, when the fridge and larder were bare. My mother would use eggs from our chickens. Swap the ham or spinach with steamed asparagus, when in season.

— Serves 2 —

2 Tbsp chopped ham or chopped cooked spinach

4 eggs

2 Tbsp heavy cream, divided

4 tsp unsalted butter, divided

Salt and freshly ground black pepper

Hot toast for serving

You will need

2 ovenproof ramekins

Preheat the oven to 350°F/175°C.

Divide the ham or spinach between the ramekins. Crack 2 eggs into each ramekin, keeping the yolks intact, then add 1 Tbsp of the cream and 2 tsp of the butter to each and season with salt and pepper.

Put the ramekins in a baking pan and carefully pour enough boiling water into the pan to reach halfway up the sides of the ramekins. Bake for 7 to 10 minutes, until the yolks are wobbling and the whites are just set.

Serve with toast.

Deviled Kidneys

To our lily-livered modern tastes, kidneys on toast—made fiery (or "deviled") with mustard, Tabasco, and Worcestershire sauce—may seem a rather, well, punchy way to start the day. But you won't be surprised to hear that Edward VII devoured these with relish. And there's little doubt they provide splendid ballast for a long day's shooting, racing, or reigning. I use lambs' kidneys, but veal are also divine.

— Serves 2 —

6 lambs' kidneys, about 12 ounces/340g total

3 Tbsp all-purpose flour

1 tsp cayenne pepper

1 tsp mustard powder

Salt and freshly ground black pepper

2 tsp unsalted butter

6 Tbsp/90ml chicken stock

A lusty jig of Tabasco sauce

1 tsp Worcestershire sauce

2 slices of white toast for serving

Snip the white cores out of the kidneys using kitchen shears and discard. Rinse the kidneys under cold running water, then drain and pat dry with paper towels.

On a large plate, use your fingers to combine the flour, cayenne, mustard powder, and some salt and pepper. Coat the kidneys in the flour mixture and shake to remove any excess.

Melt the butter in a skillet over medium-high heat and fry the kidneys for 2 minutes on each side, or until cooked.

Add the stock, Tabasco, and Worcestershire and bring to a simmer.

Remove the kidneys from the pan and keep warm. Continue to simmer the sauce for a minute or two until reduced slightly.

Serve the kidneys on toast with the sauce poured over.

Kippers

Although the kipper has long been a regular dish on the royal table, it was fried fish (whiting or sole) that was eaten more frequently. But you can't beat a good kipper, and the Duke of Windsor was so devoted to these smoked herrings that he ordered Craster kippers from Fortnum & Mason every day—to be delivered by airplane to Château de Candé in France where he lived in exile. There's nothing quite like the taste of home. Anyway, some are put off by the fiddly bones (properly filleted, there should be none) or the robustly fishy smell, which can be avoided by gently poaching in simmering water for 4 minutes. But I like them broiled, with a blob of butter gently melting on top. Manx kippers are particularly good, especially from L. Robson & Sons. For those who prefer a rather more gentle smoke, try Gloucestershire's Severn & Wye Smokery.

— Serves 2 —

2 kippers (kippered herring or split smoked herring)	2 Tbsp unsalted butter, at room temperature
Olive oil for drizzling	2 sprigs curly parsley (optional)
	1 lemon, quartered, for serving

Move a rack to the top of the oven and preheat the broiler to high. Line a rimmed baking sheet with foil, place the kippers on top with a drizzle of olive oil, and broil for 4 to 5 minutes.

Anoint the fish with butter and, if you're feeling particularly baroque, a sprig of curly parsley. Allow the butter to melt, then serve with a quarter of lemon to squeeze on top.

Rationing

1914. The start of the First World War and the beginning of the end for Edwardian excess. As rationing began to bite, King George V and Queen Mary were determined to lead from the top. Lunch would be cut to a mere three courses, and meat served no more than three times a week. Breakfast, too, was ravaged. Where once there were silver chafing dishes filled with kippers, kidneys, and kedgeree, there were now only two courses, decided by Queen Mary and ordered the night before. "If anyone was tempted to help themselves to fish when they also had sausage and bacon," remembered Gabriel Tschumi, "one look from her was sufficient to make them change their minds."

Sir Frederick Ponsonby tells the tale of one poor equerry, arriving late to breakfast and finding the table bare. He rang the bell for a boiled egg. "If he had ordered a dozen turkeys, he could not have made a bigger stir." The King accused him of being "a slave to his inside, of unpatriotic behaviour, and even went so far as to hint that we should lose the war on account of his gluttony."

Chefs in the royal kitchen tried their best to make things interesting. Fish and vegetables provided the backbone, the former fried or, in the case of smoked haddock, puréed and made into Toast Ivanhoe. Endless mutton "cutlets" (made with minced mutton and cheap filling), eggs every way, and vegetable pie did not go down well, either upstairs or down. Worse still, the King had decided that "the use of alcohol was not consistent with emergency measures for winning a war," meaning there was to be no wine served at royal meals or used in the kitchen, either. The Queen was asked what people should drink with their food. "Serve water boiled with a little sugar in the dining room," came the curt reply. And that was that.

The King was not best pleased when his Prime Minister, Lloyd George, persuaded him to go teetotal and set a good example. Despite being a moderate drinker, "I hate doing it," he wrote in his diary, "but hope it will do good." No one really seemed to care. Which annoyed the King immensely. "Balls to the whole thing," was the view of his eldest son, who also told the story of his father retiring alone to his study after dinner every night "to attend to a small matter of business." The "business" being a small glass of port.

Rationing in the Second World War was taken every bit as seriously, although the meager coupons were supplemented by game and vegetables (neither of which were rationed) from the royal estates. Fish, too, was off ration, but supply variable. The wedding breakfast, on November 26, 1947, of Princess Elizabeth and Lieutenant Philip Mountbatten was just four courses long, and over, they said, in twenty minutes. The wars may have been won. But the glory days of royal eating were forever lost.

Herrings Fried in Oatmeal

A classic breakfast dish and one much enjoyed, like most dishes, by Edward VII. Herrings are cheap, sustainable, filled with lots of lovely omega-3 fatty acids, and taste divine. What's not to love? If you can't find fresh herrings you can substitute another smallish silvery fish such as shad or sardines.

— Serves 2 —

4 herrings, cleaned and boned, heads and tails removed

5 Tbsp/75g unsalted butter, melted, plus 7 Tbsp/100g unsalted butter

Salt and freshly ground black pepper

2½ cups/250g old-fashioned rolled oats

Juice of 1 lemon

Dash of Tabasco sauce

Dip the herrings in the 5 Tbsp/75g melted butter, season with salt and pepper, then roll in the oats to coat.

Heat the remaining 7 Tbsp/100g of butter in a skillet until foaming, then add the herrings and cook for 2 to 3 minutes per side. Remove the fish from the pan to serving plates.

Add the lemon juice and Tabasco to the butter in the pan, swirl until combined and warmed through, then pour over the herrings and serve.

Haddock à l'Anglaise

Haddock, English-style. Much loved during the "Golden Age" of the English breakfast, this was just one of many fish dishes to grace the royal table. And while *à l'anglaise* can mean a multitude of different things (battered, baked, poached, grilled, and so on), it usually refers to something simply served, perhaps with a basic butter sauce. I've used smoked haddock here, as it seems more suited to breakfast.

— Serves 2 —

12 oz/340g smoked haddock or Finnan Haddie, skinned

1¼ cups/300ml whole milk

Salt

2 eggs

¼ cup/55g unsalted butter

Juice of 1 lemon

Freshly ground black pepper

Chopped fresh parsley for serving

Poach the haddock gently in the milk over medium heat until the fish is tender and warmed through, about 5 minutes. Remove the fish from the pan and quickly pat dry with paper towels. Remove and discard any bones, then cover and keep warm. Discard the remaining poaching liquid.

Bring a pan of heavily salted water to a boil. Crack each egg into a ramekin. When the water is gently boiling, create a whirlpool by stirring the water with the handle of a wooden spoon. Slide 1 egg at a time into the whirlpool, decrease the heat to a simmer, and cook the eggs until the whites are firm but the yolks are still runny. Remove the eggs with a slotted spoon and place carefully on a double layer of paper towels to drain.

Melt the butter in a small saucepan. When foaming, add the lemon juice, season with pepper, and swirl to combine.

Divide the haddock between two plates and top each serving with a poached egg. Drizzle with the lemon-butter sauce, sprinkle with parsley, and serve.

Kedgeree

Kedgeree is a breakfast classic, and one of the few Anglo-Indian dishes, along with Mulligatawny, that endures. Descended from *khichri*, an Indian lentil and rice dish, it was made English by the addition of smoked haddock (or Finnan Haddies, which some say originally came from Findon in Aberdeenshire, while others claim Findhorn in Moray). During the Second World War, the Queen Mother substituted the haddock with salmon, which was off-ration, and which she caught herself. The key is a whisper, rather than a shout, of decent curry powder, while the fresh spices and herbs add their own gentle allure.

— Serves 4 —

8 to 12 oz/225 to 340g smoked haddock, Finnan Haddie, or smoked trout, skinned

3 Tbsp olive oil

1 onion, finely chopped

1 Tbsp medium curry powder

2 green cardamom pods

1 tsp coriander seeds, toasted and ground in a spice grinder or mortar and pestle

1 tsp ground turmeric

1 fresh bay leaf

1½ cups/300g basmati rice, rinsed

2 cups/475ml chicken or vegetable stock

Salt and freshly ground black pepper

5 Tbsp/75g crème fraîche

To garnish

1 medium onion, thinly sliced

2 Tbsp unsalted butter

4 soft-boiled eggs, peeled and halved

A handful of chopped fresh cilantro

2 lemons, halved (optional)

In a large pan, combine the haddock with enough water to cover and bring to a simmer. Remove the fish and break into large pieces, discarding any bones. Set aside; discard the remaining poaching liquid.

Preheat the oven to 350°F/175°C.

Heat the oil in a heavy pot or Dutch oven over medium heat, add the chopped onion, and cook, stirring occasionally, until softened, about 10 minutes. Add the curry powder, cardamom, coriander, turmeric, and bay leaf and cook for another 5 minutes.

Add the rice to the pot and cook, stirring, for 1 minute. Add the stock, season with salt and pepper, bring to a boil, and cover. Transfer to the oven and cook until the rice is tender and all the stock has been absorbed, about 20 minutes.

Meanwhile, fry the sliced onion in the butter until golden brown, about 20 minutes. Drain on paper towels.

Remove the rice from the oven and remove and discard the bay leaf and cardamom pods. Heat the crème fraîche in a small pan, add the haddock, and cook until heated through, about 2 minutes. Gently fold the fish into the rice, then taste and season with salt and pepper, if necessary.

Transfer to a serving bowl or individual bowls and top with the fried onions, eggs, and cilantro. Serve with lemon halves, if desired.

Lunch

Lunch

Lunch. For most of us, a snatched, sorry sandwich at the desk or a rushed bowl of soup, slurped down between interminable Zoom calls. A blip, a pause, a brief stop for fuel. Which is a crying shame, because this is the most civilized of meals, one of life's true pleasures, a time to step back, sit down, and settle into a long, languorous feast, an escape from the strictures of everyday life.

And the royal family, at least in Victorian and Edwardian times, took lunch very seriously indeed. "At two o'clock came luncheon," wrote Sarah Tooley in 1897, "at which the Queen ate and drank heartily after her morning's work." But while a decent lunch these days might stretch to three courses, one eaten with Victoria or Edward VII required the stamina of an ox. "A good digestion was essential in those days," noted Gabriel Tschumi, "when each meal was equivalent to a present-day banquet. There was never any fear of Queen Victoria's guests leaving the table hungry."

Lunch would always start with a soup, either thick pottage or a clear, consommé-style broth that seemed simple enough, but required a few days preparation. Followed by fish, meat, and dishes both simple (plover's eggs, lobster salad) and more complex (*chaudfroid de poulets*); something roast (ortolans or fowls), vegetables, and at least three desserts. Along with the ever-present sideboard packed with whole cold joints of meat.

Contemporary reports of the Queen's eating habits were, as ever, flattering. "Her Majesty's tastes in food are most simple," noted an anonymous courtier. Before going on to describe her sparrow-like appetite—for lunch, little more than a tiny slice of boiled chicken, or a sliver of beef from the sirloin. The nearest our source gets to anything approaching indiscretion is that "Her Majesty confesses a great weakness for potatoes." While the Queen would not partake of every course, she was, as food historian Annie Gray points out in *The Greedy Queen*, "a woman who could eat." So all those gushing contemporary accounts of her dainty appetite should be taken with a great shovel of *fleur de sel*.

There were no such illusions about her son, Edward VII (known as Bertie to his family), who had a truly heroic appetite. And while he didn't actually drink very much—a glass or two of Chablis, or dry champagne, or claret, with the occasional whiskey and soda between meals—he most certainly could eat. For elevenses, lobster salad and cold chicken, and his ever-present thermos of turtle soup. A lunch in honor of the Shah of Iran, held on HM Yacht *Victoria and Albert*, on August 20, 1902, was typical in its glorious excess—crayfish bisque and sole mayonnaise, lamb cutlets, chicken in tarragon sauce, roast grouse, dressed crab, and cold meat in aspic, alongside various vegetables and desserts. But even this was positively spartan when compared to his "picnic" lunches for the Derby and Ascot, packed into baskets at Windsor and ferried down to the racecourse. A typical lunch, on June 19, 1908, started with cold consommé, followed by crab mousse, salmon, chicken salad, lamb cutlets, hot ham, cold quails, asparagus, Eton mess with cherries, gooseberry fool, *patisseries à la Parisienne,* and fruit. Alongside a cold buffet with pigeon pie (an Ascot tradition), cold joints of meat, salad, and rum baba. It's a wonder anyone actually managed to get up from their chair, let alone watch any racing.

But Bertie was nothing if not democratic in his tastes. While he adored the truffle-strewn voluptuousness of classic French cuisine he went from haute to hearty (roast beef and Yorkshire pudding were served every Sunday, while Irish stew, Scotch broth, and steak pies were a shooting-lunch staple) in the twitch of a whisker.

After Edward VII, things became a little, well, subdued. At York Cottage, on the Sandringham Estate, where George V and Queen Mary lived until Queen Alexandra died, one guest was astonished to turn up to lunch to find the door opened by the King, and then sitting down to a relatively parsimonious lunch of roast pheasant and chocolate mousse. George was a creature of regimented habit, supping two bowls of chicken consommé every day at 11am. On his private menus (as opposed to the more formal, French-accented ones) his tastes were simple, solid, and very British. Curries (he'd acquired a taste for them while in India) along with bluff, plain English comfort food—cutlets, cottage pie, game pie, and roast beef.

Queen Mary, though, preferred more elaborate, haute dishes such as Côtelettes de Saumon à la Montpelier. But even she rarely ate more than two courses. Their son, George VI, father of the late Queen Elizabeth, shared his father's unfussy tastes. When he came to lunch at Marlborough House with Queen Mary the menu was "fairly simple and plain," according to Tschumi, usually consisting of an omelette, chicken or cutlets, and ice cream as dessert.

The Queen Mother's lunches, at Royal Lodge at Windsor, or Birkhall in Scotland, were jolly affairs. My father remembers lobster, salmon, and "lots of things in rich, creamy sauces." Her page, William Tallon, was famously liberal with the wine. If you politely declined, putting your hand over your glass, he'd simply distract you, then top up with aplomb. Even if it meant pouring through your fingers.

The late Queen's tastes were simple. She was not, according to Mark Flanagan—royal chef to the late Queen and King Charles—a big eater and, if by herself, would often eat only one course. Queen Camilla's lunches are light: chicken consommé or smoked salmon, while the King, on the other hand, does not eat lunch at all.

The Queen Mother's
Gin & Dubonnet

Despite the vast and magnificently stocked cellars at both Windsor Castle and Buckingham Palace, the monarchs, from Queen Victoria to King Charles III, were not (and are not) great drinkers. The occasional glass, rather than endless bottles. And while the Queen Mother is affectionately remembered for liking the odd tipple—you'd certainly never go thirsty at one of her splendid lunches—it was more about being a generous host. This was a cocktail much appreciated by the late Queen and Queen Mother alike, sipped before lunch. It has a stirring mixture of sweet, bitter, and vaguely herbal flavors. And certainly puts a spring in one's step.

— Serves 1 —

2 parts Dubonnet

1 part gin

4 good ice cubes

1 lemon slice

Pour the Dubonnet, gin, and ice into a tumbler and mix well. Garnish with the lemon slice and serve.

Potage Parmentier

This recipe is a version of *Purée de Pommes de Terre, dite Parmentier,* and taken from Auguste Escoffier's *Guide Culinaire,* one of the most influential cookbooks of all time. Published in 1903, it's the bible of French haute cuisine and contains recipes inspired by the royal family, including *Cerises Jubilee* for Queen Victoria's jubilee, and *Selle d'Agneau de Lait Edouard VII.* Escoffier also cooked for Edward VII at The Savoy, among many other members of the royal family. Named after French physician and potato evangelist Augustin Parmentier, it's a classic leek and potato soup. It was also a favorite of Queen Victoria and appears on the menu of Her Majesty's Dinner in honor of her Diamond Jubilee, on Tuesday, June 22, 1897. Naturally, I've adapted the recipe slightly for the modern cook. The cream adds its usual lustrous depth, while the croutons provide crunch. To make this soup vegetarian, replace the chicken stock with vegetable stock.

— Serves 2 —

2 leeks, white parts only, cleaned and thinly sliced

2 Tbsp unsalted butter

3 medium floury potatoes, such as Russet, peeled and quartered

2 cups/475ml chicken stock

Salt and freshly ground black pepper

To garnish

Heavy cream

2 Tbsp croutons

Chopped fresh chervil or chives

In a saucepan over low heat, gently cook the leeks in the butter until softened, 10 to 15 minutes.

Add the potatoes and stock, season with salt and pepper, and bring to a simmer, cooking for 10 to 15 minutes, until the potatoes are soft to the touch.

Carefully transfer the mixture to a blender and blend until smooth.

Pour the soup into bowls, garnish with a glug of cream, the croutons, and chervil, and serve.

Queen Camilla's Chicken Soup

This is Queen Camilla's lunchtime staple. It's light yet sustaining and endlessly adaptable. In winter, carrots, thinly sliced cabbage, and potatoes provide the ballast, while in spring and summer, fava beans, peas, spinach, and green beans take their place. But feel free to throw in whatever you like, from chopped artichoke hearts, to asparagus, rutabaga, and watercress. Serve with a thick slice of toasted brown bread.

— Serves 4 —

6 cups/1.4L good-quality chicken stock

2 chicken thighs, roasted, cooled, and shredded

Juice of 1 lemon

A lusty dash of Tabasco sauce (optional)

Salt and freshly ground black pepper

Grated Parmesan cheese for serving (optional)

Winter

1 medium potato, finely diced and parboiled

1 carrot, peeled and finely diced

1 celery rib, finely diced

½ head Savoy cabbage, thinly sliced

Summer

Handful of shelled and peeled fava beans

Handful of peas (fresh or frozen)

Handful of spinach, finely chopped

Handful of green beans, thinly sliced

Bring the stock to a boil and cook until reduced by one-third, then add the chicken.

Add the potato, carrot, and celery and simmer for 3 minutes or so until tender, adding the cabbage for the final minute. If using summer vegetables, reduce the cooking time to about 1 minute.

Add the lemon juice and Tabasco (if using) and season with salt and pepper.

Pour into four bowls, sprinkle with Parmesan, if desired, and serve.

Asparagus

WITH SAUCE MOUSSELINE

In 1907, King Edward and Queen Alexandra entertained an esteemed Indian guest for dinner at Buckingham Palace. Asparagus was on the menu, as it always was when in season, served with a sauce mousseline. As they started to eat, the King noticed the man tucking in with gusto, eating the main part of the stalk, and tossing the woody stem over his shoulder. Rather than cause offense, the King quicky did the same, meaning the whole table swiftly joined in. By the end, there were numerous tiny piles of asparagus stems on the carpet behind the chairs. "There were a few grumbles from those who had to report the stains," notes Tschumi, "but there was nothing but admiration for the King's quick-wittedness." Seasonality has long been at the heart of royal eating (and, in fact, all eating before the advent of fridges and freezers), and there's much to be said for eating asparagus at the peak of its season, which starts in May and ends on the last day of Royal Ascot, sometime around mid-June. Like peas, the sugars convert quickly into starch within hours of being harvested so you want it as fresh as possible.

— Serves 4 —

24 asparagus spears, trimmed

Salt and freshly ground black pepper

For the sauce mousseline

1 cup/220g unsalted butter

4 egg yolks

½ tsp white wine vinegar

1 small ice cube

Pinch of salt

Squeeze of lemon juice

⅔ cup/160ml cold heavy cream, whipped to soft peaks

Boil or steam the asparagus in a large pan of well-salted water until tender but not soft, 4 to 6 minutes. Drain on paper towels and set aside.

Melt the butter in a pan and skim off and discard the white solids, leaving the liquid clarified butter behind. Keep warm.

In a heatproof bowl, combine the yolks, vinegar, ice cube, and salt and whisk for 1 minute. Set the bowl over a pan of gently simmering water and whisk until thick, about 5 minutes. Remove from the heat and slowly whisk in the clarified butter. When smooth and glossy, add the lemon juice.

Carefully fold the whipped cream into the sauce until homogenous. Arrange the asparagus on a serving platter or individual plates. Top with the sauce, sprinkle with black pepper, and serve immediately.

Crab Mousse

This recipe comes from "Debo," Deborah Mitford, the late Dowager Duchess of Devonshire, a remarkable woman in every way. Chicken expert, Elvis fanatic, and savior of Chatsworth House (the Derbyshire seat of the Devonshires), she was—at least to this particular child—at once terrifying, hugely glamorous, funny, and very kind indeed. She was also a dear friend of the King, and versions of this mousse have also appeared on the royal table. Don't be put off by all the ingredients (or the gelatin)—once you have the ingredients it's just a matter of putting everything together.

— Serves 4 to 6 —

¼ cup/60ml chicken, vegetable, or fish stock

1 tsp unflavored gelatin

8 to 10oz/225 to 300g good-quality lump crab meat, picked over

⅔ cup/160g mayonnaise

Pinch of cayenne pepper

Dash of Tabasco sauce

Freshly ground black pepper

6 Tbsp/90ml cold heavy cream

1 Tbsp chopped fresh chives

Thinly sliced brown toast for serving

In a small saucepan, combine the stock and gelatin and let sit until softened, about 5 minutes. Bring the mixture to a simmer and cook until the gelatin has dissolved, then set aside to cool.

In a bowl, combine the crab, mayonnaise, cayenne, and Tabasco and season with pepper. Add the stock mixture and stir to combine.

Whip the cream to soft peaks and fold into the crab mixture along with the chives. Spoon into a serving dish, cover, and chill for 3 hours, or until set.

Serve with the toast.

Potted Crab

Potting is an old English method of preservation, described as "medieval clingfilm" by food historian Bee Wilson, in which crab or brown shrimp, ham, or beef is sealed under a layer of clarified butter. I've borrowed this recipe for crab from Tom Pemberton, the chef proprietor of Hereford Road in Bayswater, London. Simply because it's the best I've ever tasted. Crabs are available all year round but are at their best between March and November.

— Serves 6 —

12 Tbsp/175g unsalted butter, divided

1 lb/450g good-quality lump crab meat, picked over

⅛ tsp freshly grated nutmeg

Pinch of cayenne pepper

Pinch of ground mace

Juice of ½ lemon

Salt and freshly ground black pepper

For serving

Toast

Cucumber pickles (optional)

You will need

6 ramekins

Melt 5 Tbsp of the butter. In a large bowl, combine the crab with the melted butter, nutmeg, cayenne, and mace, and gently fold to combine. Here, two kitchen tropes are relevant: taste as you add and taste again. The amounts are only guides—they cannot account for personal preference, or the age or strength of the spices used. Also, add incrementally—you can always add but you can't take away.

Fold in the lemon juice and season with salt and pepper, then taste again and adjust the seasoning, adding lemon juice accordingly. Divide the mixture among the ramekins and smooth the tops with the back of a spoon, then cover and refrigerate for 30 minutes.

Place the remaining 7 Tbsp of butter in a small pan over low heat. When the fats and solids start to separate, remove from the heat before the butter browns. Pour into a glass measuring cup and let rest until the milky solids have sunk to the bottom, then carefully spoon off the yellow clarified butter from the top and pour over the potted crab to seal. Cover and chill for at least 1 hour, until set.

Eat within three days and enjoy with toast and, if you like, cucumber pickles to cut the richness.

Crab with Sauce Remoulade

There are surprisingly few, if any, crab recipes in the books of Francatelli and Escoffier. Perhaps it was seen as the poor cousin of the more noble lobster (although I'm not sure why) and thus seen as unfit for royal bellies. But by the time Edward VII reached the throne it had scuttled onto center stage, where it remains to this day. This dish was served to George V at Ascot on June 16, 1922. You can make your own mayonnaise, which is not hard. But because the flavors here take no prisoners, Hellmann's is just fine.

— Serves 2 —

8 oz/225g jumbo lump crab meat, fresh if possible

Thinly sliced white toast for serving

1 lemon, quartered, for serving

For the sauce remoulade

1 cup/240g mayonnaise

2 Tbsp Dijon mustard

1 Tbsp finely chopped capers

1 Tbsp chopped gherkins

1 Tbsp finely chopped fresh tarragon

1 Tbsp finely chopped fresh parsley

3 anchovy fillets, drained and finely chopped

Freshly ground black pepper

Mix all the sauce ingredients together and season with pepper.

Divide the crab between two plates and add a dollop of the sauce to each plate. Serve with thin white toast and a squeeze of lemon.

Lobster Salad

Another summer classic, found as often at Ascot lunches and Royal Opera House dinners as it was at Castle of Mey lunches and picnics with the Queen Mother. Of course, lobster doesn't come cheap, so this is somewhat of a treat.

— Serves 2 —

1 medium lobster, cooked, hewn in half, tail meat removed and cut into 1 inch/2.5cm medallions, knuckles cracked and meat removed, claws tapped with the back of a heavy knife so the flesh can be easily slipped from the shell

1 lemon, quartered, for serving

For the sauce

⅔ cup/160g mayonnaise

3 Tbsp ketchup

Dash of Tabasco sauce

Dash of Worcestershire sauce

Pinch of cayenne pepper

Dash of brandy

For the salad

3 heads baby gem lettuce, cored and sliced into strips

1 avocado, pitted and diced

½ cucumber, seeded and diced

2 tomatoes, peeled, seeded, and diced

Salt

For the dressing

3 Tbsp extra-virgin olive oil

2 Tbsp white wine vinegar

1 Tbsp freshly squeezed lemon juice

Salt and freshly ground black pepper

Combine all of the sauce ingredients in a large bowl. Reserving the claws, add the remaining lobster meat to the sauce and mix well.

In a second bowl, combine the lettuce, avocado, cucumber, and tomato and season with salt.

Add all of the dressing ingredients to a mason jar, season with salt and pepper, then cover and shake to combine. Toss the dressing with the salad and divide between two cocktail glasses.

Spoon the lobster mixture on top of the salad and garnish each serving with a claw. Serve with lemon quarters.

Smoked Eel Mousse

This recipe comes from Gavin Rankin, the ever-elegant proprietor of Bellamy's in Mayfair, which was one of the late Queen's favorite restaurants. She had impeccable taste. Now try as I might, Gav is far too discreet to tell me what she ordered. "She might have eaten the smoked eel mousse more than once, but that is something that I can neither confirm nor deny." In fact, Gavin didn't come up with the actual recipe. He leaves all the cooking to his marvelous executive chef, Stéphane Pacoud, while this particular patron gets on with the serious business of *mange*-ing *ici*. If you don't have seafood consommé (few do), feel free to use a shellfish or fish stock. It won't taste quite as rich, but saves an awful lot of bother.

— Makes 6 —

2 Tbsp water

1½ tsp unflavored gelatin, divided

1 cup/240ml cold heavy cream

8 oz/225g smoked eel or trout fillets, skinned

6 Tbsp/90g mayonnaise

½ cup/120ml seafood consommé, cold or room temperature (or fish, lobster, or shrimp stock)

Toast for serving

You will need

Six 3-inch/7cm ramekins

In a small bowl, combine the water with ¾ tsp of the gelatin and let sit until softened, about 5 minutes. Microwave until bubbling and the gelatin has dissolved, about 15 seconds. Let cool slightly. Whip the cream to soft peaks, then add the gelatin mixture and continue to beat until the mixture holds stiff peaks.

In the bowl of a food processor, combine the eel and mayonnaise and process until very fine, scraping down the bowl with a rubber spatula as needed. Transfer to a bowl and fold in the whipped cream.

Fill the ramekins three-quarters full with the mousse, smoothing the tops with the back of a spoon, and let chill in the fridge for 1 hour.

Meanwhile, in a small saucepan, combine the consommé with the remaining ¾ tsp of gelatin and let sit until softened, about 5 minutes. Bring the mixture to a simmer and cook until the gelatin has dissolved. Let cool to room temperature. Add enough of the consommé mixture to each ramekin to measure about ¼ inch/6mm deep (about 3 tsp). Return to the fridge until set, at least 1 hour. Serve with thin, white toast.

Truites Froides au Rubis

This sea trout dish was served at Edward VII's Epsom lunch party in 1909. A mustard-keen racing man, it was the year that his horse, Minoru, won the Derby, making him the first reigning British monarch to achieve this legendary accolade. There is no bigger race to win in the world, so that day must have been very jolly indeed. Lunches both at Ascot and Epsom were typically lavish affairs. I tend to avoid salmon these days, as the farming industry is both environmentally ruinous and produces a pretty second-rate fish, too. Sea trout is far superior in every way to the sad, flabby, and fatty farmed beasts. To keep stocks sustainable, sea trout is not available in the UK during the closed season (November 1 to April 2), so if you're cooking this during the colder months, use farmed trout instead.

— Serves 8 —

1¾ cup/415ml dry white wine

1 celery rib, sliced

1 small leek, white and green parts, quartered

1 onion, thickly sliced

1 lemon, quartered

2 bay leaves

½ bunch parsley, stems included

½ tsp whole black peppercorns

6 cups/1.4L water

1 whole sea trout or Arctic char, about 4½ lb/2kg, cleaned, with head and tail left on

2 egg whites plus the egg shells, roughly crushed

¾ cup/175ml full-bodied red wine

2 Tbsp unflavored gelatin

To garnish

6 eggs, at room temperature

¼ cup/60g mayonnaise

Salt and freshly ground black pepper

3 tomatoes, peeled and diced

¼ cucumber, seeded and diced

Dill sprigs

In a fish kettle (see Note on page 50), combine the white wine, celery, leek, onion, lemon, bay leaves, parsley, and peppercorns. Add the water, bring to a boil, then reduce the heat and simmer for 5 minutes. Remove from the heat and let sit for 30 minutes to allow the aromatics to infuse the court bouillon.

Place the fish in the pan, adding more water if necessary to ensure the fish is at least half submerged, and slowly bring to a boil. Cover and simmer for about 30 minutes, until the fish is cooked through. Remove from the heat and let the fish cool in the pan.

When cool, carefully lift the fish from the pan and remove the skin and fins, leaving the head and tail intact. Cover and chill for at least 2 hours.

continued overleaf

While the fish is chilling, strain the cooled court bouillon into a clean pan.

In a small bowl, whisk the egg whites until foamy and add to the court bouillon along with the egg shells. Slowly bring to a boil over medium heat without stirring. Simmer for 1 minute, then remove from the heat and let sit for 5 minutes. At this point the egg whites will have cooked and risen to the top of the court bouillon, forming a crust or raft trapping all the impurities and oil.

Using a large spoon, carefully make a hole in the middle of the crust and slowly ladle the resulting clear stock into a fine-mesh sieve lined with a double layer of cheesecloth set over a clean bowl. Pour into a pitcher or glass measuring cup—you will need just shy of 4 cups/900ml. Add the red wine and mix to combine. Cover and let cool, then chill until completely cold.

In a small saucepan, combine ⅔ cup/160ml of the chilled court bouillon mixture with the gelatin and let sit until softened, about 5 minutes. Bring the mixture to a simmer and cook until the gelatin has dissolved.

Add the gelatin mixture back to the remaining court bouillon and whisk to combine. Chill until the mixture is thickening and just starting to set.

Pat the trout dry with paper towels, place on a large tray, and slowly spoon one-third of the gelatin mixture over the body of the fish, leaving the head and tail uncovered. Return to the fridge for 30 minutes to set.

Repeat this process two more times with the remaining gelatin mixture, chilling in between layers, until the fish is enrobed in a layer of jelly. (If the pouring gelatin mixture sets a little too firmly to spoon, simply warm to the correct consistency, being careful that it is not hot, otherwise it will melt the first layers of jelly already on the fish.) Let set for at least 1 hour and then transfer the fish to a serving platter.

Meanwhile, for the garnishes, cook the eggs in boiling water for 10 minutes to hard boil. Cool under cold running water, then peel and halve. Press the yolks through a fine-mesh sieve, mix with the mayonnaise, and season well with salt and pepper. Pipe or spoon the yolk mixture back into the egg white halves. Garnish the trout with the eggs, tomatoes, cucumber, and dill sprigs and serve.

Note: If you don't have a fish kettle, double line a very large roasting pan with heavy-duty aluminum foil, allowing extra to drape over the sides. Add the fish poaching ingredients and simmer as per the recipe, then leave to cool and infuse. Reheat the court bouillon, add the fish, cover tightly with foil, and cook in a 300°F/150°C oven for about 30 minutes, until cooked through. Let cool in the pan and proceed with the recipe as written.

Salade Aida

This is a classic Escoffier salad, also made by Francatelli for Queen Victoria. A rare moment of crisp, green respite in the midst of all that butter and cream.

— Serves 4 —

4 endives, preferably red, cored and leaves separated

4 artichoke bottoms, sliced ¼ inch/6mm thick (or 12 canned artichoke hearts, drained and sliced)

2 green bell peppers, stemmed, seeded, and sliced ¼ inch/6mm thick

4 eggs, boiled for 8 minutes, peeled, and halved

For the dressing

6 Tbsp/90ml good extra-virgin olive oil

2 Tbsp red wine vinegar

1 tsp Dijon mustard

Salt and freshly ground black pepper

Arrange the vegetables in a large bowl. Remove the yolks from the boiled eggs, slice the egg whites and add to the bowl, then crumble the yolks and scatter on top. Add all of the dressing ingredients to a mason jar, season with salt and pepper, then cover and shake well until emulsified. Gently toss the dressing with the salad and serve.

Oeufs Suzette

This was a dish served to George V, recovering from septicemia and an abcess on his lung, when convalescing in the brisk Bognor sea air. "Bugger Bognor" were said to be his last words, uttered in response to his doctor, who promised that he would soon be well enough to recuperate in the Sussex seaside town. If only it were true. The reality is rather more prosaic. The people of Bognor had asked if they could rename the town Bognor Regis, in honor of his stay. "Bugger Bognor," he growled to his private secretary, Arthur Stamfordham. Nevertheless, their wish was granted. Convalescent dishes were plain and easily digestible, involving all manner of beef jellies, chicken custards, and a thousand ways with eggs. Despite the simplicity of these dishes their preparation was usually anything but. The original recipe contains béchamel sauce, but with all the butter and cream involved it's an embellishment too far.

— Serves 4 —

4 medium Russet potatoes, scrubbed

7 Tbsp/100g unsalted butter

½ cup/120ml whole milk

6 Tbsp/90ml heavy cream

Salt and freshly ground black pepper

8 thin slices of ham

4 eggs, poached (see page 25)

Handful of shredded Gruyère or Comté cheese

Crisp green salad for serving

Preheat the oven to 425°F/220°C.

Bake the potatoes for about 1 hour, until the skins are deep brown and crisp. When cool enough to handle, slice off the tops and scoop the flesh out into a bowl, and reserve the skins. Add the butter, milk, and cream, season with salt, and mix well.

Heat the broiler to high.

Line the inside of each potato shell with two slices of ham, then spoon the potato mixture back into the shells, leaving a 2 inch/5cm gap at the top of each. Top each potato with a poached egg, sprinkle with cheese, and broil. Top with black pepper and serve with a crisp green salad.

Fish Goujons

WITH TARTAR SAUCE

Another timeless and eternal royal favorite, this is fried fish with a thick French accent. Dover sole would have been traditionally used, but it does seem an awful waste. I tend to use haddock or plaice but even pollack, that rather dreary but eminently sustainable fish, will do.

— Serves 4 —

For the goujons

3 slices slightly stale hearty white sandwich bread, crusts removed, torn into 1-inch pieces (or 1½ cups panko breadcrumbs)

¾ cup/105g all-purpose flour

Sea salt and freshly ground black pepper

2 eggs, beaten

1 lb/450g skinless white fish fillets, such as cod, haddock, plaice, pollack, or sole, cut into 1- to 1½-inch strips

3 Tbsp olive oil

1 lemon, cut into wedges, for serving

For the tartar sauce

½ cup/120g mayonnaise

Pinch of mustard powder

1½ Tbsp finely chopped capers

2 Tbsp finely chopped cornichons

1 small shallot, finely chopped

1 Tbsp chopped fresh flat-leaf parsley

Combine all of the sauce ingredients in a bowl and set aside.

Add the bread to the bowl of a food processor and pulse to make crumbs, then spread them on a plate. On a second plate, season the flour with salt and pepper and mix with your fingers. Put the eggs in a shallow dish. Using one hand (this stops both hands getting clagged up), dip the fish strips into the flour, then the egg, then the breadcrumbs, shaking off any excess at each stage.

Heat the oil in a large skillet over medium-high heat. When hot, fry the fish in batches until crisp and golden, then drain on paper towels. Keep hot while cooking the rest.

Serve with the lemon wedges and a great big dollop of tartar sauce.

Salmon Fishcakes

This was a typical lunch dish for Queen Elizabeth II, always made with salmon and mashed potato, then dipped in breadcrumbs and fried in butter. Once done, a "neat circle" would be sliced from the top and a small indentation made to allow a poached egg to sit snugly on top. Hollandaise sauce was then poured over. For a breakfast version, substitute half of the salmon with smoked haddock.

— Serves 4 —

1 lb/450g Yukon Gold potatoes, boiled until soft, cooled, and peeled

3 Tbsp salted butter, softened and divided

6 Tbsp/90ml whole milk

Salt and freshly ground black pepper

12 oz/340g boneless, skinless salmon fillet

Splash of white wine

2 tsp ketchup

Handful of chopped fresh flat-leaf parsley

Grated zest of ½ unwaxed lemon

3 Tbsp all-purpose flour, seasoned with salt and pepper

2 eggs, beaten

1 cup/110g fine dried breadcrumbs

4 eggs, poached (see page 25)

1¼ cups/300ml hollandaise sauce (omit the heavy cream from the Sauce Mousseline recipe on page 39)

Peas for serving

Make mashed potato by passing the cooked potatoes through a potato ricer into a bowl, then beat in 1 Tbsp of the butter and the milk. Season with salt and pepper and set aside.

Preheat the oven to 425°F/220°C.

Place the salmon on a large piece of aluminum foil, add the wine, season with salt and pepper, then wrap into a loose parcel and place on a rimmed baking sheet. Bake for 10 minutes, then remove, open the parcel, and let cool.

Flake the salmon into the mashed potato and add the ketchup, parsley, and lemon zest. Mix well, then form the mixture into four round cakes.

Put the flour, eggs, and breadcrumbs into three separate bowls. Dip each cake first in flour, then into the eggs, and finally the breadcrumbs.

Heat the remaining 2 Tbsp of butter in a heavy skillet until foaming, then gently fry the cakes for about 5 minutes on each side, until golden. Remove to a plate lined with paper towels. Slice the top of each fishcake off and make an indention in the exposed surface.

Place a poached egg on top of each fishcake, drown in hollandaise sauce, and add freshly ground black pepper before serving with the peas.

Bounty from the Royal Estates

"In spite of the vast resources at her command for the raising of food under artificial conditions," wrote an anonymous courtier, of Queen Victoria, "she never permits her own table or that of Her Household to be served with anything that is out of season." Royal menus, whether private or public, have always been in thrall to the seasons. Through necessity, in Victorian times. And then, as ice boxes transformed into freezers, and fresh fruit began to fly in from across the world, for the pure delight of eating food at its very peak—asparagus in May, strawberries in June, grouse in August, or pheasant in October. That annual wait made everything taste that much the sweeter. It still does.

Game has long been central to the royal diet, with grouse and venison from Balmoral, pheasant and partridge from Sandringham, and rabbit, snipe, hare, and blackcock from various royal lands across the country. Wild salmon was caught on the Dee, and trout in freezing mountain lochs. The estates have always provided all the fruit and vegetables, too—Windsor in particular. The glass houses at Frogmore in Victoria's day were a magnificent sight. She had eight "pineries"—hothouses in which pineapples, the very apotheosis of exotic and extravagant eating (it took many thousands of pounds to produce just one fruit) were grown throughout the year. There were 250 different varieties of pear and the same of apples, 2,220 yards of outdoor asparagus beds, and an astonishing five miles of peas. Some 130 gardeners worked full time to keep kitchens supplied and mighty appetites sated.

These days, things are a little more modest, although the royal kitchens still very much depend on the seasonal bounty of their farms and estates. The royal farm at Windsor, which supplies the palace kitchens as well as the farm shop, has a Sussex beef herd, a Jersey dairy herd, lambs, chickens, and pigs. The late Queen even had her own double-cream cheese made exclusively for her. King Charles has long been known for his passionate support of British food and farming. In fact, there has never been a sovereign with such a close and fundamental connection to the land. He was preaching for the seasonal, local, and sustainable many years before they became the norm. And is not only fluent in the rural tongue, but a successful farmer himself. The link between land and sovereign is as strong as ever.

Poached Trout & Langoustine Salad

This salad was part of lunch at Buckingham Palace after the Coronation of Charles III, a particularly merry feast. We were mighty relieved (if not at all surprised) that this magnificent ceremony had gone so well. ChalkStream farmed trout is one of my favorite suppliers, as the fish are raised in waters with fast-flowing, clear water, meaning they don't have the usual muddy taste.

— Serves 8 to 10 —

One 1½ lb/680g skinless ChalkStream trout, Arctic char, or salmon fillet (see Note)

20 to 30 fresh langoustines (live is best, if you can find them) or 1 lb/450g extra jumbo (16/20) shrimp, peeled, tailed, and deveined

10 quail eggs, or 5 chicken eggs

4 oz/115g mixed leaf salad (depending on the season, I like to include a variety of strong-flavored leaves: arugula, mizuna, and watercress with added herbs such as chervil and dill)

8 oz/230g green beans, cooked

5 oz/140g mi-cuit or sunblush tomatoes or 4 oz/115g oil-packed sun-dried tomatoes, torn into bite-size pieces

1 lemon for zesting

For the citrus vinaigrette

1 Tbsp freshly squeezed lemon juice

1 Tbsp freshly squeezed orange juice

1 tsp white wine vinegar

1 tsp Dijon mustard

¼ cup/60ml extra-virgin olive oil

Salt and freshly ground black pepper

For the court bouillon

1¾ cups/415ml dry white wine

1 celery rib, sliced

1 small leek, white and green parts, quartered

1 onion, thickly sliced

1 lemon, quartered

2 bay leaves

½ bunch parsley, stems included

½ tsp whole black peppercorns

6 cups/1.4L water

In a large pot or high-sided skillet, combine all the court bouillon ingredients, bring to a boil, then decrease the heat and simmer for 5 minutes. Remove from the heat and let sit for 30 minutes to allow the aromatics to infuse.

Gently poach the trout in the court bouillon for about 10 to 20 minutes, until the flesh is opaque. Carefully remove and allow to cool until you can gently handle it, mindful that the trout will be fragile.

Add the langoustines (or shrimp) to the court bouillon in batches and boil for 2 to 4 minutes. They are ready when the flesh on the undersides is white rather than

continued overleaf

translucent. Remove from the pan and stop the cooking by refreshing in ice water, but do not leave in cold water. Peel and set aside.

Cook the quail eggs in the court bouillon for 3 minutes (or 8 minutes for chicken eggs). Remove and set aside.

To make the citrus vinaigrette, lightly whisk all of the ingredients together in a small bowl or shake together in a mason jar, seasoning with salt and pepper to taste.

Gently toss the salad leaves and herbs with three-quarters of the vinaigrette and arrange on a platter. Gently flake the trout into quite large, succulent pieces and arrange on and around the salad leaves. Season the langoustine tails (or shrimp) with most of the remaining vinaigrette, ensuring they are well coated, and scatter over the salad. Add the green beans and tomatoes. Peel the eggs and slice in half, then dot around the salad. Use a rasp-style grater to finely grate a little lemon zest over the top of the salad to finish. Serve with extra vinaigrette on the side.

Note: While ChalkStream trout are a kind of rainbow trout, they are much more akin to fatty, red-fleshed Arctic char or salmon than they are to American rainbow trout.

★

Grilled Sardines

Ah, the sweet scent of sardines grilling over coals, their salt-flecked skins blistering to reveal that rich flesh within. I'm not alone in my adoration. In 1925, the *Victoria and Albert* (the royal yacht with a crew of 300 and household staff of 30) sailed through the Mediterranean, starting at Genoa and on to Naples, Syracuse, Etna, and Palermo, before sailing back to where they started. "Every day we had sardines for luncheon," recalls Tschumi. King George V grew very fond of these Mediterranean sardines and they were regularly served at Buckingham Palace.

— Serves 4 —

16 sardines, gutted and scaled	Salt
Olive oil	1 lemon, quartered, for serving

Either heat a charcoal grill to the point where the coals have a thin layer of white ash on top, heat a gas grill to high, or whack up the broiler to maximum level.

Anoint the fish with olive oil and season well with salt. Cook on the grill or under the broiler for 2 to 4 minutes per side, depending on size. Serve with a squeeze of lemon.

Halibut en Papillote

This was another dish served after the Coronation of Charles III. It was the most momentous of days, but that lunch was surprisingly laid back (well, as laid back as lunch can be in Buckingham Palace), and very happy, too.

— Serves 4 —

2 Tbsp cold unsalted butter, plus room temperature butter for greasing

½ lemon, zested then sliced

½ cup/60g sliced shallots

1 bay leaf

2 large sprigs tarragon

½ star anise

Four 4 oz/115g skinless, boneless halibut fillets

Salt and freshly ground black pepper

¾ cup/175ml dry white wine

¾ cup/175ml fish stock

½ cup/120ml heavy cream

Finely chopped tomato and snipped chives for garnish

For serving

Buttered new potatoes and seasonal vegetables (such as wilted spinach, fava beans, baby carrots, or asparagus)

Preheat the oven to 350°F/175°C.

Take a large sheet of aluminum foil, fold it in half to strengthen it, and place on a rimmed baking sheet. Generously butter the foil, then scatter with half of the zest and lemon slices and shallots, adding the bay leaf, one tarragon sprig, and the star anise. Top with the halibut fillets, season with salt and pepper, then cover the fish with the remaining zest and lemon slices, shallots, and tarragon. Ensuring the edges of the foil form a slight bowl, add the wine and fish stock, then cover with another sheet of foil and roll up the edges to create a sealed packet, being careful not to make any tears or holes in the foil.

Bake for 8 to 10 minutes, during which time the fish will have steamed and the foil puffed up to create a pillow. Remove from the oven and let sit for 3 to 4 minutes. (Be careful of the steam when opening.)

Carefully remove the fish from the packet then strain the cooking liquid into a saucepan and bring to a gentle boil. Add the cream and reduce to a thick sauce that just coats the back of a spoon. If necessary, thicken with a few knobs of the cold butter. Adjust the seasoning before serving.

Garnish the fish and sauce with the tomatoes and chives and serve with buttered new potatoes and a selection of seasonal vegetables.

Saumon Chambord

The edible equivalent of Ozymandias's mighty boast, "Look on my works, ye Mighty, and despair!" Invented by Francatelli, it was one of those extravagant showstoppers that not only proclaimed the genius and technical ability of the chef, but also used a glut of extravagant ingredients. Just, I suppose, because he could. A whole salmon was poached in champagne before being skinned, speared by four crayfish, then girded with Dover sole fillets studded with truffles. At its base, whole black truffles, whiting quenelles stained pink by lobster coral, more crayfish, and mackerel roe, all covered in Espagnole sauce and lashings of anchovy butter. Subtle, it ain't. It would have originally been made with wild salmon, one of the most magnificent of fish; lean, muscular, and packed with flavor. The farmed version, though, is a sorry shadow of its noble cousin, not just flabby and pretty second rate, but environmentally ruinous, too. I try to avoid it at all costs, but in writing a royal cookbook it's nigh on impossible to ignore. Either use Arctic char, or go for the best-quality farmed fish you can find. I've slightly simplified the recipe (just for a change).

— Serves 4 —

Four 6 oz/170g center cut skin-on salmon fillets, pin bones removed

12 oz/340g small chestnut mushrooms, trimmed (or small crimini or button mushrooms)

4 shallots

2 sprigs thyme

2 bay leaves

Salt and freshly ground black pepper

1¾ cups/415ml dry red wine, preferably Burgundy

1 cup/240ml fish stock

¼ cup/55g unsalted butter, diced and divided

1 Tbsp all-purpose flour

4 herring roes (optional, but recommended)

1 fresh black truffle, thinly sliced (very much optional)

Preheat the oven to 350°F/175°F. Place the salmon fillets in a baking pan lined with aluminum foil. Coarsely chop half of the mushrooms and all of the shallots and add to the pan with the fish. Add the thyme and bay leaves and season with salt and pepper. Pour in the wine and fish stock to almost cover the salmon. Cover and bake for about 25 minutes, until the fish is just cooked. Carefully lift the salmon from the pan and remove the skin, then cover and keep warm.

Strain the cooking liquid into a saucepan, bring to a boil over medium heat, and cook until reduced by half.

In a small bowl, mash together 2 tsp of the butter with 2 tsp of the flour to make a smooth paste. Add the butter mixture to the simmering sauce a little at a time, whisking constantly, until the sauce is smooth and has thickened slightly.

Whisk another 1 Tbsp of the butter into the sauce over low heat until the sauce is smooth and glossy.

Melt the remaining butter in a skillet, add the remaining whole mushrooms, and cook over medium-high heat until browned and tender. Remove from the pan and keep warm.

If using the herring roes, season the remaining 1 tsp of flour with salt and pepper and use it to coat the herring roes. Add to the hot pan and cook for about 30 seconds on each side, until golden and cooked through.

Place the salmon on plates and divide the mushrooms and herring roes among them. Spoon over some sauce, keeping the remainder for serving, and finish with sliced truffles, if desired. Serve with the extra sauce.

Fried Sole

WITH SHRIMP SAUCE

Dover sole, along with turbot and salmon, has been a mainstay of royal menus from Victoria onwards. Escoffier had hundreds of ways with Dover sole, but this recipe, adapted from one by Francatelli, advises using smaller specimens, as the big buggers are "less likely to appear crisp, so essential a requisite in all fried fish." The original recipe involves a shrimp sauce made with industrial amounts of butter and flour. I prefer things a little lighter, so have removed the flour and cut down on the dairy. Lemon, slip, or megrim sole would be perfect. You need to ask the fishmonger to gut and skin them, and trim the fins, too.

— Serves 2 —

¾ cup/105g all-purpose flour, seasoned with a big pinch of salt and few twists of black pepper

2 eggs, beaten

1 cup/110g fine or panko dried breadcrumbs

¼ cup/60ml olive oil

½ cup/110g unsalted butter

2 medium sole (lemon, megrim, or slip)

For the shrimp sauce

½ cup/110g unsalted butter

70g (or one packet) brown shrimp, or 4 oz/115g peeled, tailed, raw pink shrimp, halved lengthwise then cut into ½-inch/1.3cm pieces

Juice of ½ lemon

Pinch of cayenne pepper

1 anchovy fillet

Pinch of salt

Place the seasoned flour, eggs, and breadcrumbs in three separate bowls.

Heat the oil and butter together in a large skillet over medium heat until the butter starts to foam.

Dip the soles in the flour, then into the egg, then the breadcrumbs. Place in the pan and fry for 4 to 6 minutes on each side, depending on size, until the skin is crisp and golden.

For the sauce, melt the butter in a saucepan over medium heat until foaming, then add the shrimp, lemon juice, cayenne, anchovy, and salt. Cook gently for a few minutes, then pour over the sole and serve. (If using pink shrimp, cook, stirring, over medium-low heat until opaque, 2 to 4 minutes.)

Poulet Danoise

Queen Mary certainly knew her onions. Yet she also disliked "extravagance of any kind and it displeased her if food at Marlborough House was ever wasted." Not unlike her granddaughter and great grandson. This dish was her favorite. Tschumi suggests making your own "nouilles" or noodles, but fresh tagliatelle will do fine, or even decent-quality dried stuff.

— Serves 4 to 6 —

1 large chicken, about 4 lb/1.8kg

Salt and freshly ground black pepper

1 large onion, sliced

2 carrots, peeled and roughly chopped

1 bay leaf

1¼ cups/300ml chicken stock (made with a decent bouillon cube is fine)

1¼ cups/300ml heavy cream

Juice of ½ lemon

12 to 16 oz/340 to 450g fresh tagliatelle (or other decent-quality dried pasta)

Unsalted butter for the pasta

For the flavored butter

14 Tbsp/200g unsalted butter, softened

2 Tbsp chopped fresh parsley

Juice of 1 lemon

Preheat the oven to 350°F/175°C.

For the flavored butter, mash the butter with the parsley and lemon juice, then put half inside the cavity of the chicken and smear the other half all over the outside of the bird. Season well with salt and pepper.

Put the chicken in a roasting pan along with the onion, carrots, and bay leaf. Roast for about 1 hour 45 minutes, or until the juices run clear when you pierce the thickest part with the tip of a knife. (Make sure it doesn't brown too much, so cover with aluminum foil if it is browning too quickly.)

Take the chicken out and set aside to rest. Strain the juices through a fine-mesh sieve into a clean saucepan, skim off most of the fat, then add the stock and cream and simmer to reduce. Season with lemon juice, salt, and pepper.

Cook the pasta according to the package instructions then drain, toss with a little butter, and transfer to a serving platter.

Carve the chicken and lay on top of the pasta, then cover with the sauce and serve very hot.

Chicken Salad

This is a take on the classic chicken salad, eaten from Queen Victoria's day onwards. The good thing about a chicken salad is its adaptability, to both whim and season. Add what you want, remove what you don't. The usual royal recipe includes a great slick of mayonnaise, but I prefer the sharper, more subtle allure of a good vinaigrette.

— Serves 4 —

1 whole chicken (about 2½ lb/1.1kg), roasted (with lemon in cavity and heavily seasoned) for 1 hour, then rested for 20 minutes

¼ cup/55g unsalted butter

4 garlic cloves, finely chopped

4 thick slices sourdough bread, cut into ¾ inch/2cm cubes

4 small heads romaine lettuce, cored and leaves separated

6 tomatoes, sliced

One 14 oz/400g can artichoke hearts in oil, drained

12 anchovy fillets

4 soft-boiled eggs with jammy yolks, halved

For the dressing

6 Tbsp/90ml white wine vinegar

1 Tbsp Dijon mustard

1 Tbsp mustard powder

Salt and freshly ground black pepper

1¼ cups/300ml extra-virgin olive oil

Roast your chicken first and leave it to rest.

For the dressing, put the vinegar, Dijon, mustard powder, and a pinch each of salt and pepper into a bowl and whisk. Slowly add the oil and whisk until emulsified. Set aside.

Heat the butter in a skillet until foaming, then add the garlic and cook gently until soft. Add the bread and fry until crisp. Remove the croutons with a slotted spoon to drain on paper towels.

Tear the chicken into good-sized chunks, making sure you get every last bit of meat off the bones. (Reserve the carcass for stock.) Place the chicken meat in a large serving bowl then add the lettuce leaves, tomatoes, artichokes, anchovies, croutons, and eggs. Mix well, then lavish with the dressing, ensuring every last bit is coated. Serve with extra dressing on the side.

Trio of Curries

The royal family have long been fans of a curry. But it's important to point out that these are very much anglicized recipes, more similar to the British curry house staples—which bear scant relation to the real thing—than the regional dishes of India, Pakistan, and Bangladesh. That said, Victoria's Indian servants roasted and ground their own spices, as well as killed their own animals in accordance with religious law. So while the monarch's tastes were very westernized, Victoria's Indian attendants could cook and eat the real food of their homeland.

Elizabeth II's Curry

The late Queen was a curry lover, but her tastes, according to her Royal Chef Mark Flanagan, were assuredly mild. "With the curry recipe for the late Queen Elizabeth," Mark Flanagan tells me, "we adapted a rather standard 'British-style' curry recipe using a generic curry powder. Her Majesty preferred not to take chili, or anything particularly spicy. Coconut was also a flavor that was not enjoyed. So we used to finish the curry using a more fragrant garam masala to elevate the base, using spices such as cinnamon, saffron, and cardamom, then adding in natural yogurt and some freshly chopped flat-leaf parsley instead of cilantro. As important as the curry," he continues, "were the condiments and accompaniments—these always included some diced cucumber, chopped tomato, mango chutney, well-cooked chopped shallots, some poppadoms, and additional natural yogurt (just in case)." You can buy garam masala, but it always tastes so much better when you make it yourself. Just store in an airtight container out of the light.

— Serves 4 —

¼ cup/60ml vegetable oil

4 green cardamom pods

2 bay leaves

2 onions, finely chopped

1½ Tbsp ground coriander

1 tsp ground turmeric

1 Tbsp mild curry powder

1 heaped Tbsp all-purpose flour

2 cups/475ml chicken stock or water

8 boneless, skinless chicken thighs

3 Tbsp full fat Greek yogurt

Pinch of sea salt

Pinch of saffron

Handful of fresh flat-leaf parsley, chopped

2 tsp garam masala (see opposite)

For the garam masala

1 Tbsp green cardamon pods,
husks cracked

1½ cinnamon sticks

½ tsp whole cloves

1 tsp cumin seeds

1 tsp coriander seeds

For serving

Steamed or boiled basmati rice

½ cucumber, peeled and diced

2 tomatoes, peeled and finely diced

¼ cup/60g full fat Greek yogurt

8 poppadoms

3 Tbsp mango chutney

2 shallots, sliced and fried in oil until
brown and crisp, then drained on
paper towels

To make your own garam masala, dry roast all the ingredients in a heavy pan over medium heat until you smell the oils being released. Put into a spice grinder or mortar and pestle, grind, then store in an airtight container.

To make the curry, heat the oil in a large pan, then add the cardamom pods and bay leaves and cook until they crackle and pop. Add the onions and cook for about 15 minutes, until soft, then add the coriander, turmeric, curry powder, and flour and stir well.

Add the stock gradually, stirring to make a sauce, then add the chicken, yogurt, salt, and saffron. Simmer gently for 20 to 25 minutes, until the chicken is cooked through.

Stir in the parsley and garam masala and cook for a couple more minutes, then retrieve the cardamon pods and bay leaves and discard.

Serve with basmati rice and other accompaniments.

Pictured overleaf

Francatelli's Chicken à l'Indienne, George V's Curry, and Elizabeth II's Curry (clockwise from top left)

George V's Curry

"King George V had far simpler tastes than his father," writes Tschumi, "and we had heard that as Prince of Wales he had shown little interest in any kind of food, except curry and Bombay duck, of which he was extremely fond, for the King had developed a taste for it in India." It was not served when he had guests, but the King "made it quite clear to M. Cedard [his head chef] that he did not see why it should not be provided for him at private luncheons. We made it from meat, game or chicken, depending what meat was available, but the King's favourite curry was one made from beefsteak and served with Bombay duck." Bombay duck is a particularly ugly species of lizard fish, pink, with a great gaping mouth, eaten fresh or sun-dried and salted. Hugely popular in Parsi and Bengali cuisine, as well as Gujarati, in coastal Maharashtra, Goa and Karnataka, along with Sri Lanka and Bangladesh, it's cooked into stews, curries, gravies, bhajis, and chutneys. You can buy it online.

— Serves 4 —

8 chicken thighs, on or off the bone (Tschumi also used rabbit or pheasant, and you could use stewing beef, too, a favorite of George V)

7 Tbsp/100g unsalted butter, divided

3 large onions, chopped

1 garlic clove, crushed

2 cooking apples, peeled, cored, and chopped

8 large tomatoes, peeled, seeded, and chopped

3 Tbsp curry powder

1 Tbsp chili powder

1 bay leaf

4 cups/950ml good chicken stock

1 cup/80g unsweetened shredded coconut

Juice of 1 lemon

½ cup/120ml heavy cream

For serving

Steamed white basmati rice

Dried, fried Bombay duck, crumbled (optional)

Chopped fresh cilantro (optional)

In a heavy pot or Dutch oven, brown the chicken in 3½ Tbsp of the butter. Remove from the pot and set aside.

Add the remaining 3½ Tbsp of butter to the pot and gently fry the onions, then the garlic, then the apples, and finally the tomatoes, until cooked but not browned. Stir in the curry and chili powders.

Meanwhile, put the bay leaf, stock, and coconut in a separate pan and bring to a boil. Strain the stock and add to the pot with the vegetables, then continue to cook for 10 minutes.

Add the chicken to the sauce skin-side up and simmer gently for 45 minutes. Remove the chicken and set aside. If the sauce is still too thin, reduce further.

Strain the sauce through a fine-mesh sieve and return to the pot, then add the lemon juice and cream. Simmer until it reaches a "good thickness," then return the chicken to the sauce. Simmer over low heat for 10 minutes.

Serve with basmati rice and Bombay duck and cilantro, if desired.

Francatelli's Chicken à l'Indienne

This is a Frenchman's take on an Indian curry. But not one eaten by Queen Victoria herself because hers were, according to Tschumi, "the special province of her Indian cooks and servant," who killed their own sheep and poultry for the curries for "religious reasons," as well as grinding their own curry powder between two large round stones and preparing their own spices. The curries were always served by "two Indians in the showy gold-and-blue uniforms worn at lunchtime." But when her son, Edward VII, ascended to the throne he dispensed with their services and curries were cooked in the royal kitchen. I've adapted this for the modern cook, replacing the "cook's meat curry paste" with curry powder.

— Serves 4 —

8 boneless, skinless chicken thighs

7 Tbsp/100g unsalted butter, divided

3 large onions, sliced

4 garlic cloves, chopped

3 celery ribs, sliced

1 blade of mace (optional)

4 whole cloves

3 Tbsp medium curry powder

1 tsp chili powder

1½ cups/360ml chicken or vegetable stock

In a large skillet, fry the chicken thighs in 3½ Tbsp of the butter until well browned all over. Remove from the pan and set aside.

Add the remaining 3½ Tbsp of butter to the same pan and gently cook the onions, garlic, celery, mace, cloves, curry powder, and chili powder until the vegetables are softened.

Add the stock, mix well, then return the chicken to the pan skin-side up. Simmer gently for 45 minutes, or until the chicken is cooked through, before serving.

Both pictured on previous pages

Duck with Stewed Peas

The original recipe uses duckling, slowly stewed, and was a Francatelli favorite, often on his menus for Queen Victoria. But I've borrowed Mark Hix's recipe because I love the way the richness of the confit duck goes with the sweetness of the peas.

— Serves 4 —

4 duck legs

8 oz/225g duck fat

4 garlic cloves, unpeeled

10 black peppercorns

5 whole cloves

1 bay leaf

2 tsp sea salt

1 large Russet potato, cut lengthwise into four ½- to ¾-inch/1 to 2cm thick slices

For the peas

1½ cups/200g shelled English peas, preferably fresh

Salt

1 tsp sugar

Grated zest and juice of 1 small orange

Handful of pea tendrils (pea shoots) or small salad leaves

Preheat the oven to 350°F/175°C. With a heavy knife, chop the knuckles off the duck legs, then cut around the thigh bone with the point of the knife, ensuring you don't go through the skin, and chop the bone just below the knuckle. Fold the thigh in and push the drumstick meat down to expose the bone so each looks like a little ham. Pack the legs into a tight-fitting pan, then add the duck fat, garlic, peppercorns, cloves, and bay leaf. Sprinkle with the sea salt then cover and bake in the oven for 1 hour, or until the legs are soft but not falling apart.

Increase the oven temperature to 400°F/200°C. Lay the potato slices in an ovenproof skillet, then remove the duck legs from the fat and place one leg on top of each slice of potato. (You can strain the excess duck fat into an airtight container and keep it in the fridge to use at a later date.) Transfer to the oven and bake 30 to 35 minutes, until the fat is crisp. (You may want to put a little foil on the leg bones to prevent them from burning.)

Meanwhile, cook the peas in boiling salted water with the sugar for 4 to 5 minutes, until tender, then drain.

To make the dressing, put the orange zest and juice in a bowl and whisk in 1 Tbsp of the liquid duck fat.

To serve, use a spatula to remove the duck legs on their potato slices and transfer to serving plates. Arrange the stewed peas and pea tendrils around the duck and spoon around the dressing.

Shooting

"Shooting was certainly one of my father's greatest pleasures in life," remembered the Duke of Windsor. "For him the magic period from August to January meant glorious days on the moor, or 'on the hill' in Scotland, or matching his skills with other famous 'guns' during the partridge and pheasant seasons in England." George V was one of the great shots of his era, as elegant as he was deadly. Although "bags" (the term used to cover the number of birds shot) back then were notably excessive.

At the peak of the "big shoots," in the years preceding the outbreak of the First World War, over 20,000 head of game were shot per year at Sandringham alone, while bags of 2,000 birds, shot by eight guns in a day, were not uncommon. Of course, every bird was picked, hung, plucked, and devoured with barely a scrap wasted. But these numbers were more slaughter than sport. Especially as the pheasants at Sandringham weren't exactly renowned for their speed or height.

Perhaps the bloodthirsty peak was reached in 1913 at Hall Barn, the home of Lord Burnham, owner of the *Daily Telegraph*. "My father was deadly that day," recalled David, his eldest son, "and used three guns." As the light faded and the "carnage" stopped, the bag was announced: 3,937 birds, and George had shot 1,000. Even he was troubled by the numbers. "Perhaps we went a little too far today, David," he said to his son on the drive back to London.

Thankfully, those days are long gone, and the rather awful spectacle of mass slaughter of unsporting birds is no longer considered acceptable. Quite right, too. Shooting can only be justified if birds are killed cleanly. And eaten. Grouse is the first to appear on the menu on the "Glorious Twelfth" of August. When young, its flesh is sweet and elegant, softly scented with heather. Then partridge; from September 1st, the native English gray-leg birds possess far more flavor than the "Frenchies," or reared red legs. Pheasant season begins in October, which coincides with the peak of the deer-stalking season. All three game birds, along with venison, were very much the seasonal stars of every royal menu from Victoria to the present day.

In fact, Balmoral was bought as a shooting estate by Prince Albert who loved stalking deer. Shooting lunches at Sandringham, under Edward VII, took place in a field within a vast tent, the floor swept and covered in straw. A royal standard fluttered above. Tables were clad in thick linen and formal crockery while guests feasted upon mulligatawny soup, steak, kidney and lark pudding, and roast pheasant. Lunches these days are a whole lot less extravagant: a chicken pie, perhaps, or Irish stew. And the shooting is very much about conservation, the preservation of the countryside, and supporting the rural economy rather than obscenely senseless slaughter.

Partridge Hotpot

Mark Flanagan was royal chef to the late Queen and now to His Majesty King Charles III, and a very fine cook he is, too. As well as having the patience of Job, he has an ability to stay cool under immense pressure, whether cooking a state banquet for 180 people, lunch for four, or a diplomatic reception for 1,000. He's also an incredibly nice man. This recipe comes from *A Royal Cookbook: Seasonal Recipes from Buckingham Palace*, a book he wrote alongside Edward Griffiths. It makes use of the partridge, a game bird that comes into season at the start of September. Although the reared, red-legged (or "French") partridge is more common, the far rarer wild and native English gray leg has a better flavor.

— Serves 4 —

1¾ lb/800g Yukon Gold potatoes, peeled and sliced ¼ inch/6mm thick

Salt and freshly ground black pepper

2 Tbsp vegetable oil, divided, plus more as needed

4 oven-ready partridges (if partridge is unavailable, poussins will do, or 8 boneless chicken thighs)

14 oz/400g sausage meat, casings removed if necessary

1 onion, diced

2 carrots, peeled and cut into ¾-inch/2cm pieces

2 leeks, white parts only, cleaned and cut into ¾ inch/2cm pieces

⅔ cup/160ml dry cider

4 sprigs thyme

1 bay leaf

2 cups/475ml game or chicken stock, plus more as needed

2 Tbsp unsalted butter

Preheat the oven to 350°F/175°C.

Parboil the potatoes in a large pan of lightly salted water until just tender but still holding their shape, about 5 minutes. Drain and let cool.

Heat 1 Tbsp of the oil in a heavy ovenproof pot or Dutch oven over medium heat. Season the partridges with salt and pepper and brown for about 4 minutes, turning often, until golden all over. Transfer to a plate and set aside.

Roll the sausage meat into twelve neat balls, add to the hot pot, and brown well all over, adding a little more oil if needed. Remove and set aside with the partridges.

Add the onion, carrots, and leeks to the pot along with the remaining 1 Tbsp of oil, decrease the heat, and cook, stirring often, until the vegetables are softened but not browned, about 5 minutes.

Meanwhile, cut the legs from the partridges and slice the breast meat away from the remaining bone (reserve the carcasses to make stock or soup). Pick out any visible shot.

Add the cider, thyme, and bay leaf to the pot and bring to a boil, then add 1½ cups/400ml of the stock. When the liquid has returned to a boil add the partridge and sausage meat and season with salt and pepper. Add a little more stock, if needed, to just cover the meat.

Cover the mixture with the potato slices, overlapping slightly, and dot with the butter. Bake for 35 to 40 minutes, until the potatoes are tender and golden brown.

★

Venison Stew

Game has always been central to royal food, and venison—along with grouse, partridge, and pheasant—is a staple. This is a big, hearty sort of dish, served at shooting lunches and family lunches alike. Edward VII was a particular fan, as was his son, George V, and it was made using deer they had shot at Balmoral. If you don't have venison, beef will do.

— Serves 4 —

Olive oil for browning

1¾ lb/800g venison, diced

2 onions, diced

2 celery ribs, diced

2 carrots, peeled and diced

2 garlic cloves, finely chopped

1 Tbsp red currant jelly

1¼ cups/300ml dry red wine

2 cups/475ml beef stock

A good glug of Worcestershire sauce

1 bay leaf

1 tsp chopped fresh thyme

Salt and freshly ground black pepper

Mashed potatoes for serving

Preheat the oven to 300°F/150°C.

Heat a good glug of oil in a heavy ovenproof pot or Dutch oven over high heat and brown the venison in batches. Remove and set aside.

Add a little more oil to the pot along with the onions, celery, and carrots. Decrease the heat to medium and cook for about 10 minutes, stirring often, until soft and lightly browned. Add the garlic and cook for 2 minutes.

Increase the heat, add the jelly and wine, and deglaze the pot, stirring until the boozy aroma has gone. Return the venison to the pot, add the stock, Worcestershire, bay leaf, and thyme, and season well with salt and pepper.

Bring to a boil, then cover and transfer to the oven, and cook for about 3 hours, or until the meat is spoon-soft. Serve with mashed potatoes.

Scotch Broth

You can't go wrong with a Scotch broth. Simple, soothing, and cheap to make, it shows that the tastes of the royal family could be resolutely down to earth. It was served regularly at Balmoral from the reign of Queen Victoria onwards. This recipe comes from that Scottish genius, Jeremy Lee. I love his cooking as much as I love him.

— Serves 6 —

2½ lb/1.1kg lamb scrag end or neck fillet

¼ cup/50g pearl barley, rinsed

3 medium carrots, peeled and trimmed

2 medium onions

2 medium potatoes, peeled

1 rutabaga, peeled and trimmed

7 oz/200g baby turnips (if available), peeled and trimmed

3 leeks, white parts only, cleaned and trimmed

1 small head cabbage

1 bay leaf and 1 sprig thyme, tied with kitchen twine

Sea salt and freshly ground black pepper

Cut off any large chunks of fat on the meat. Place the meat in a large, heavy pot or Dutch oven and cover with water. Bring to a boil and skim off any impurities that rise to the surface. Add more water to make up for that lost through evaporation and skimming, then return to a boil and decrease the heat to a simmer. Add the barley.

Cut the vegetables into small cubes and add to the pot, starting with the carrots and finishing with the leeks and cabbage. (Some fresh spring vegetables—new potatoes, peas, fava beans, et al.—enhance the dish immeasurably but these should be added to the pot no more than 20 minutes before serving). Add the herb bundle, season with salt and pepper, and let the broth tick away for 2 hours. Keep skimming any foam that rises to the surface.

Remove and discard the herb bundle before serving. (It can be served right away but tastes much better the next day.)

Irish Stew

In March 1899, the soon-to-be Queen Mary departed for Nice to stay with Queen Victoria at Cimiez, "sustained by Irish stew, which was made at Windsor and kept tepid by being wrapped in red flannel cushions." It was also a shooting lunch staple from the reign of Edward VII onwards.

— Serves 4 to 6 —

2 middle necks of lamb, filleted, boned and bones reserved (you could also use 3 lb boneless lamb shoulder or 4.5 lb bone-in lamb shoulder, but it does need to have some extra fat, as this is a slow-cooked dish)

8 cups/1.9L lamb or beef stock (see Note below)

12 oz/340g carrots, peeled

1 lb/450g Russet potatoes, peeled

1 lb/450g Yukon Gold potatoes, peeled

1 onion, thickly sliced

Pinch of fresh thyme leaves

Salt and freshly ground black pepper

Chopped fresh chives and flat-leaf parsley for serving

Cut the lamb into large chunks and put in a heavy pot. (Traditionally, the meat is not browned.) Add the stock and bring to a boil, skimming off all the impurities from the surface. Remove the lamb with a slotted spoon and reserve. Strain the stock through a fine-mesh sieve into a clean pot. Return the lamb to the stock and bring to a boil, then decrease the heat, cover, and simmer gently for 30 minutes.

Meanwhile, cut the carrots into pieces slightly smaller than the lamb and the potatoes into pieces the same size as the lamb. Add the carrots, Russet potatoes, and onion to the pot, return to a boil, then cover and simmer for 20 minutes. Next, add the Yukon Gold potatoes and thyme, return to a boil and simmer, partially covered, until the lamb and carrots are tender and the Russet potatoes have broken down and thickened the stew, 20 to 30 minutes.

Remove from the heat, cover, and let sit without stirring for 15 minutes.

Season with salt and pepper, then serve sprinkled generously with chives and parsley.

Note: Ask your butcher to bone the lamb for you and have them give you the bones, too. Make a well-flavored stock using the bones and the trimmings from the carrots and onion, plus other vegetables and herbs you like.

Roast Rib of Beef

Roast rib of beef. As much an edible representation of England as it is stalwart of the Sunday lunch table. "Oh! The Roast Beef of England, And old English Roast Beef," roared Henry Fielding, novelist and author of *The Grub Street Opera*, his red-blooded paean to the joys of roasted meat and patriotism. "When mighty Roast Beef was the Englishman's food, it ennobled our brains and enriched our blood." And despite Edward VII's love of haute French cuisine, he also adored good old-fashioned English food. Roast beef with roast potatoes, Yorkshire puddings, and lashings of gravy was a stalwart of the Sandringham table. And served every Sunday night at Buckingham Palace, too. Buy the best beef you can afford, preferably from a good butcher. Rare breed beef can be wonderful, from Belted Galloway and White Park to Hereford and Aberdeen Angus, but producing amazing beef is so much more than just breed. It's a complex juggling act of feed, finishing, ageing, and butchery. The production of great beef takes knowledge, experience, and a lot of hard work.

— Serves 6 —

3 Tbsp olive oil

8 to 10 lb/3 to 4 kg whole, bone-in rib of beef

Worcestershire sauce for sprinkling

2 Tbsp mustard powder

Sea salt and freshly ground black pepper

Preheat the oven to 475°F/245°C.

Massage the oil into the beef, then sprinkle with Worcestershire sauce, then mustard powder. Season lustily with salt and pepper, then transfer to a roasting pan. Roast for 20 minutes, then decrease the oven temperature to 375°F/190°C and roast for an additional 10 minutes per 8 oz/225g of meat for rare.

Let rest in a warm place for 20 minutes before carving and serving.

The Special Relationship

President Franklin D. Roosevelt was a man who not only enjoyed his food, but knew its power, too. "A gourmet with an instinct for people's hidden motivations," wrote historian Alex Prud'Homme, "FDR researched what his guests liked to eat, drink and smoke, then constructed a menu that was more than a simple list of things to eat. It was a meal layered with signs and symbols." One morning in 1938, he read about a planned visit by George VI and Queen Elizabeth to Canada. Ostensibly a goodwill Commonwealth tour, there was a more important ulterior motive—to galvanize support against the rise of Nazi Germany.

FDR had seen Hitler's threat from afar, but the USA had little appetite for getting involved in another expensive, far-off war. Especially one supporting the British, whom many Americans still resented. But if FDR could persuade the King and Queen to visit the USA, then perhaps public opinion would soften. He wrote to the King, asking them for "three or four days of very simple country life at Hyde Park [the Roosevelts' home in upstate New York]—an opportunity to get a bit of rest and relaxation." The King accepted his invitation.

Despite successful visits by Edward VII and the Duke of Windsor (both as Prince of Wales), this was the first time a reigning British sovereign had set foot in the USA. And so in June 1939, the King and Queen found themselves sitting on folding chairs at Hyde Park, eating hot dogs served on silver platters. The King seemed a little nonplussed. "What should I do?" he asked the President. "Put it in your mouth and keep chewing until you finish it," came the smiling response. "King Tries Hot Dog And Asks For More," cried the headline of *The New York Times*. "And He Drinks Beer With Them." The American public were delighted, seeing the royal couple as homely and down-to-earth rather than frosty, former imperial overlords. Behind the scenes, the King and FDR discussed the Nazi threat, with the President promising to defend British Atlantic convoys and sink German U-boats. In 1941, Roosevelt sent his troops into battle. That lunch became known as the "picnic that won the war."

Queen Elizabeth II made four official state visits over her reign, to Presidents Dwight D. Eisenhower, Gerald Ford (New England lobster, stuffed saddle of veal), George Bush (Maine lobster, crown roast of lamb), and George W. Bush (pea soup, Dover sole, saddle of spring lamb). But it was her relationship with President Reagan, with their shared love of horses, that was the warmest. Her trip to the Reagans' Rancho del Cielo, just outside Santa Barbara, California, in March 1981 was drenched in torrential rain more suited to Scotland than the West Coast. They ate enchiladas, chile rellenos, refried beans, and guacamole. Quite what Her Majesty thought of her vibrantly spiced lunch we'll never know. But one thing is for certain. Whatever her view, she would have pronounced it "delicious."

FDR's Hot Dogs

These are the hot dogs that played a starring role in "the picnic that won the war" (see page 92). And while I'd never dare, as an Englishman, to wade into the debate as to the superiority of New York (steamed onions, mild mustard) over Chicago (chopped raw onion, yellow mustard, green relish, a dill pickle spear, peppers, and celery salt) or Washington (half-smoked dog, chili, mustard, and onions), I do prefer raw onion to cooked.

— Serves 4 —

8 frankfurters (the best you can find—apparently, FDR served a local brand: Swishers)

8 hot dog buns

For serving

Ketchup

Mustard

Chopped raw or fried onions (optional)

Bring a pan of water to a boil, then simmer the frankfurters for 3 minutes. Drain on paper towels.

Split and toast the buns, add the frankfurters, and top with your condiments of choice.

Quiche de Lorraine

There have been endless egregious sins committed in the name of this French regional classic. Most of them by supermarkets, with their sullen frisbees of fridge-cold, inedibly sorry stodge—the very definition of drab dyspepsia. Elizabeth David once described the quiche as a "culinary dustbin," and a quick glance at some of the more appalling versions—with canned salmon or asparagus tips, shriveled mushrooms, and sweaty, processed ham—prove her point. There was even a tongue-in-cheek Eighties bestseller called *Real Men Don't Eat Quiche*. But proper Quiche Lorraine—a glorious combination of flaky pastry, and wobbling, just-set custard, studded with crisp shards of smoky bacon—is something we all can love, a markedly superior tart. It featured quite heavily on the royal menus, but more as a savoury, a dish eaten between the main course and dessert. Tschumi has a recipe that is described as "The Duchess of Gloucester's Savoury," but it's very much a bite-size delight, and omits the bacon. This recipe is taken from the late, great Keith Floyd. He may not have been French, but red Burgundy certainly pulsed through his veins. His version is particularly purist, omitting even the Gruyère. Feel free to throw a generous handful into the egg and cream mix.

— Serves 4 to 6 —

1½ cups/210g all-purpose flour, plus more for dusting

7 Tbsp/100g cold unsalted butter, diced, plus 2 tsp for topping

Salt and freshly ground black pepper

7 Tbsp ice water, plus more as needed

1 tsp white wine vinegar or lemon juice

6 oz/170g smoked bacon, diced

4 eggs, beaten

2 cups/475ml heavy cream

You will need

8-inch/20cm fluted tart tin with 2-inch/5cm high sides with a removable base or a regular pie plate

Pie weights or dried beans

To make the pastry, add the flour and the 7 Tbsp/100g butter to a bowl. Using your fingers or a pastry cutter rub the butter into the flour until the texture is of fine sand with only small flecks of butter remaining. Season well with salt, then add the water and vinegar and mix to combine using a spatula and adding more water as needed to bring the mixture together. Knead lightly to gather the dough into a ball, flatten into a disc, cover, and chill for 1 hour.

Lightly dust the counter with flour, roll out the pastry, and carefully transfer it to the tart tin, easing it into the corners until evenly lined. Prick the bottom all over with a fork and chill while you preheat the oven to 375°F/190°C.

Line the pastry shell with aluminum foil, fill with pie weights, and bake for 25 minutes. Remove the foil and weights and cook for a further 8 to 10 minutes to dry out the base.

Meanwhile, fry the bacon until crisp, remove from the pan, and leave to drain on paper towels. In a bowl, beat together the eggs and cream and season well with salt and pepper.

Increase the oven temperature to 400°F/200°C. Place the tart tin on a rimmed baking sheet then sprinkle the bacon into the tart shell, pour in the cream mixture, and dot the top with little pieces of the remaining 2 tsp of butter. Bake for about 25 minutes, until golden brown and set.

Serve warm or at room temperature.

Tea

Tea

Tea, that most British of mid-afternoon pursuits. Not the drink, although that plays a central role. But the one royal constant that has barely changed from the days of Victoria. She was a particular fan, thanks to her not being allowed to partake growing up, save as a "great treat" in teenage years. Despite not having a sweet tooth, I love a proper tea. Sandwiches, crusts cut off, spread thick with butter and filled with slices of good ham, heavy on the mustard; smoked salmon, egg salad, and roast beef. There are crumpets, hot and dripping with more butter, lavished with Marmite or honey. And cakes of every hue and flavor. British food may get an international (and totally unwarranted) kicking, but no one can argue the eternal appeal of a proper tea.

Victoria, according to a courtier, had a "strong weakness for afternoon tea." Even when out on the Scottish moors, John Brown and the other gillies would boil a kettle in some "sheltered corner" while the Queen and young princesses sketched. "This refreshing cup of tea has ever ranked high in the Royal favour." The confectionery cooks at Windsor were kept busy all year as their role was "principally to supply the Queen's tea table." Her favorites included "chocolate sponges, plain sponges, wafers of two or three different shapes, langues de chat, biscuits and drop cakes of all kinds, tablets, petits fours, princess and rice cakes, pralines, almond sweets, and a large quantity of mixed sweets." So much for that delicate appetite.

Little wonder she had quite the reputation as a lover of cake. "It is known that the Queen of England eats macaroon cakes continually," wrote the poet Edward Lear, who had once taught her drawing, "and she also insists on her suite doing the same." After devouring two scones, two pieces of toast, and a few biscuits, she commented to Lady Lytton in 1897 "I'm afraid I must not have any more." Such restraint was not the norm. According to her granddaughter, Princess Maud of Wales, she even dunked her cake in tea, in the German style. And would "take tea" at the summerhouse, Adelaide Cottage, or Swiss Cottage at Windsor, writing in her journals that she "found" or "took" tea, which, as Annie Gray points out, was "something of an over-simplification of what was often quite a convoluted process with a fair degree of planning and catering involved."

Served at five on the dot, it was (and still is) the most relaxed of royal meals, a time for Edwardian (if not Victorian) women to remove their uncomfortable, tightly laced corsets and slip into a tea dress, loosely fastened. This was the time when the patisserie chefs could really flex their culinary muscles, with eclairs, Chelsea buns, financiers, pralines, and cakes from lemon to chocolate and fruit. At Sandringham, Edward VII would appear, dressed in a short black jacket and black tie. And, accompanied by the merry tunes of his band, would dig into poached eggs, petit fours, rolls, cakes hot and cold, scones, preserved ginger (good for the digestion!), and "that particular species of Scotch shortcake," writes the historian Christopher Hibbert, "of which he was especially fond." Tea at the other palaces was equally expansive.

After the death of George V (another enthusiastic eater of tea), Queen Mary moved to Marlborough House where she lived alone. Yet Gabriel Tschumi records how "she abetted me in the business of providing cakes or biscuits for her young grandchildren." On Monday, November 12, 1951, she noted in her menu book, which was shared with the chef, that the Duke and Duchess of Gloucester would be coming to tea along with their son, Prince Richard. The menu ran as follows: "Bridge rolls aux oeufs et cresson. Sandwiches saumon fumé; biscuits (home made); ginger cake; chocolate cake; sponge cake iced. Bread and butter." The next day, the book returned, with messages alongside, written in her elegant hand. The smoked salmon sandwiches were deemed "excellent."

The late Queen also had a full afternoon tea every day. If it were just her and Prince Philip, there were always sandwiches, scones (never dressed), pastries, and biscuits, both homemade and shop bought, the Praline Choco-Leibniz being a favorite. As well as a large "cutting" cake, a Genoise chocolate sponge, a Victoria sponge, or Rich Tea chocolate biscuit cake.

With guests, at Balmoral or at Windsor, more savory dishes would be added: potted shrimps, sardines on toast, or a special tea purée, made from game, to be spread on toast. If children were coming, a special effort would be made to make things more fun.

In the case of Charles III and Queen Camilla, it's still a 5pm ritual where we all gather together at a round table in the drawing room at Birkhall after an afternoon spent outside mushroom hunting. Or, in my case, buying secondhand cookbooks in nearby Ballater's brilliant Deeside Books.

There are always cakes, usually one chocolate and one fruit, along with flapjacks, occasional potted shrimps, crumpets in winter, and, best of all, sandwiches. On a good day, I can put away a dozen. A good tea is a great thing. But an extra meal, however lovely, doesn't do wonders for the waist.

Afternoon Tea Sandwiches

Sandwiches are the high point of any serious tea, buttered lavishly, crusts cut off, and sliced into fat fingers. Don't stint on the filling. The Queen Mother's Mayonnaise would have been in constant use in the Queen Mother's kitchen, and is a recipe that I've adapted from a rather wonderful book called *The Royal Blue & Gold Cook Book*.

— All recipes make 6 finger sandwiches —

Smoked Salmon

¼ cup/55g salted butter, softened

4 slices soft brown bread

4 oz/115g good smoked salmon (Severn and Wye, Secret Smokehouse, John Ross, and Daylesford are my favorites)

Generous squeeze of lemon juice

Freshly ground black pepper

Spread the butter on one side of each bread slice to fully coat, then layer the salmon onto the buttered sides of two of the slices. Squeeze over some lemon juice and grind on some black pepper. Place the remaining two slices of bread on top, buttered-sides down, then slice off the crusts and cut each sandwich into three fingers.

Ham & Mustard

¼ cup/55g salted butter, softened

4 slices soft white farmhouse bread

4 oz/115g good-quality sliced ham (preferably York—the dry, proper stuff, not slimy, processed rubbish)

Big dollop of Colman's English mustard (or Dijon mustard)

Spread the butter on one side of each bread slice to fully coat, then layer two slices of ham onto the buttered sides of two of the slices of bread.

Add a thin layer of mustard to the buttered sides of the remaining two slices of bread and place them on top, buttered-sides down. Slice off the crusts and cut each sandwich into three fingers.

Egg Salad

¼ cup/55g salted butter, softened

4 slices soft white farmhouse bread

For the egg salad

4 eggs, boiled for 8 minutes and peeled

3 Tbsp of the Queen Mother's Mayonnaise (or use store-bought if you must)

Dash of Tabasco sauce

Handful of chopped fresh chives

Splash of white wine vinegar

Pinch of sea salt

A big screw of freshly ground black pepper

For the Queen Mother's Mayonnaise (makes about 2½ cups/590ml)

3 fresh egg yolks, at room temperature

1 tsp Dijon mustard

Salt

2⅓ cups/545ml vegetable oil

2 Tbsp white wine vinegar mixed with a pinch of chopped tarragon, plus more vinegar as needed

To make the Queen Mother's Mayonnaise, beat the yolks with the mustard and a pinch of salt until thick and lemon colored. Gradually whisk in the oil by droplets until it forms a creamy but firm mixture. Whisk in the vinegar mixture. (It is very important to continue beating the sauce while adding the droplets of oil and vinegar. If using the mixer or blender, mix on high speed, being sure that all ingredients are well blended to achieve a thick substance.) Once combined, taste and season with salt and vinegar if necessary. This makes more than enough for sandwiches but will keep in the fridge in a clean jar for up to 2 weeks.

To make the egg salad, place the eggs in a bowl and mash with a fork, then stir in the mayonnaise, Tabasco, chives, vinegar, salt, and pepper.

Spread the butter on one side of each bread slice to fully coat. Spoon 2 Tbsp of egg salad onto the buttered sides of two of the slices, then place the remaining two slices of bread on top, buttered-sides down. Slice off the crusts and cut each sandwich into three fingers.

Pictured overleaf

*Ham & Mustard,
Smoked Salmon, and
Egg Salad Sandwiches
(clockwise from top left)*

Coronation Chicken Sandwiches

I know, I know, it really wouldn't be a royal cookbook without this so-called regal "classic," officially known as *Poulet Reine* Elizabeth. It was created in 1953 by Constance Spry and Rosemary Hume and served at the late Queen's Coronation lunch. Now the original version, as below, is perfectly civilized, but as the years went on all manner of base and vile things were done to this perfectly innocent recipe: adding almonds and raisins, lashings of turmeric, and God knows what else until it became a banana-hued, sickly-sweet aberration, the abject filling for a thousand sorry gas station sandwiches. Originally made with poached whole chicken, I've made things a little easier by using poached breast, and have left out the heavy cream. I've also replaced the apricot purée with mango chutney.

— Makes 12 sandwiches —

2 boneless, skinless chicken breasts	1 bay leaf
1 onion, chopped	Juice of 1 lemon, plus more as needed
2 Tbsp olive oil	2 Tbsp mango chutney
2 tsp curry powder	1¼ cups/300g mayonnaise
1 tsp tomato paste	Salt and freshly ground black pepper
6 Tbsp/90ml dry red wine	8 slices brown bread
½ cup/120ml water	Salted butter, softened, for spreading

Put the chicken breasts in a pan of water, bring to a boil, and simmer for 10 to 15 minutes, or until the juices run clear from the thickest part of the breast. Allow to cool, then shred.

Fry the onion in the oil over medium heat for about 10 minutes, until soft, then add the curry powder and cook for 2 minutes. Add the tomato paste, increase the heat, then add the wine and cook to burn off the alcohol. Add the water, bay leaf, and lemon juice and simmer gently for 10 minutes.

Remove from the heat and strain through a fine-mesh sieve, pressing on the solids to extract as much liquid as possible, then discard the solids. Let the sauce cool.

When the sauce is cool, add the chutney and mayonnaise and mix well. Season to taste with salt and pepper and add more lemon juice if needed.

Mix the chicken with the sauce.

Butter four of the bread slices on one side, spreading to fully coat, then top each generously with the chicken mixture and finish with the remaining four slices of bread, pressing down gently. Remove the crusts and cut each sandwich into three fat fingers.

Potted Shrimp

ON CRUMPETS

Potted shrimp is the most English of dishes. Tiny brown shrimp (and they are the only crustacean we call "shrimp," rather than "prawn") with the very sweetest of flavors are covered in butter spiced with mace, bay, and cayenne pepper. Potting is an old preservation technique. At Buckingham Palace and Windsor, there was usually some form of potted meat, beef and chicken in particular, perfect for picky and hearty eaters alike. This really is the simplest recipe, but if you can't be bothered to make your own, then the best brown potted shrimp come from Morecombe Bay, in Lancashire. You can also buy them ready-made from the great Baxters. This is a dish I've eaten at Birkhall for tea, as well as for a starter at dinner. Or just as a deeply civilized snack. Serve cold on brown toast, or melted, as below, onto hot crumpets.

— Serves 6 —

¾ cup/170g unsalted butter

1 tsp freshly ground black pepper

¼ to ½ tsp cayenne pepper

½ tsp ground mace or freshly grated nutmeg

1 small bay leaf

1 lb/450g cooked, peeled brown shrimp, coarsely chopped or 1 lb/450g peeled, tailed, raw pink shrimp, cut into 1/2-inch/1.3cm pieces

Salt

For serving

6 crumpets, toasted

2 lemons, cut into wedges

You will need

6 ramekins

Melt the butter in a saucepan then add the black pepper, cayenne pepper, mace, and bay leaf. Add the shrimp and stir to coat. Cook for a couple of minutes, until warmed through (if using pink shrimp, cook over medium-low heat until cooked through and opaque, 5 to 7 minutes), then remove from the heat. Remove and discard the bay leaf and season with salt.

Divide the shrimp mixture among the ramekins and season with a little salt. (The butter should fully cover the shrimp.) Chill in the fridge until set.

Pile high onto hot crumpets and serve with lemon wedges.

Picnics & Barbecues

"The Queen always had a passion for eating in the open air, and has retained her taste for so doing until the present day." So wrote an anonymous courtier, who then went on to describe, somewhat breathlessly, how Queen Victoria once made a "delightful luncheon" on the moors above Balmoral, consisting of "warmed-up broth and potatoes which she helped boil herself." With the "help" of a servant or two, no doubt. Seminal moments in royal history aside, both Victoria and Albert were enthusiastic al fresco feasters. And rarely set forth on a walk, stroll, stalk, or shoot without a wicker basket filled with thermoses of tea and a couple of fortifying fruit cakes.

And it's at Balmoral that the picnic tradition continues to this day. The Queen Mother was a picnic maestro and, according to her biographer William Shawcross, "nothing gave her more pleasure than picnics and they happened almost every day, rain, snow or shine." The food was simple, but "fun, especially the jam puff and cream pastries which would explode all over the faces of the uninitiated."

The late Duke of Edinburgh was renowned as a grill master, and he designed all of his own kit, including a portable grill with three different racks that can be moved up and down for absolute grilling precision. It is a work of barbecue art. As is his picnic trailer, made to be towed behind a Land Rover, with lots of different compartments for everything from spices and herbs to tools, plates, and cutlery. Form and function. Everything has its exact place, and woe betide the poor guest who put the mustard and ketchup in the drawer meant for tongs. Edward VII had his own specially designed hotbox, used for transporting food from kitchen to shooting picnic. It was used for George V's visit to France during the First World War.

Prince Philip would have made a fine engineer, and chef, too. "The Duke was truly interested in food, and was a hugely talented cook," Mark Flanagan told me. "He was a genuine gourmet, but never a snob. It was all about the flavor, and it didn't need to be complicated or overly fussy. He was a very unfussy man." At Balmoral, he'd suddenly appear in the kitchen in search of that night's dinner: Well-hung venison, grouse, a sirloin of beef, or sausages. "He would then have his own marinade, and always had a firm idea of what he wanted to cook that night. It was an honor and pleasure to work for him." His youngest son, Edward, now Duke of Edinburgh, has taken over barbecue duties, although from my own recent experience Peter Phillips, son of the Princess Royal, has certainly inherited his grandfather's way with fire. Those Balmoral barbecues still burn bright.

Queen Mary's Cheese Biscuits

These are little savory cracker-like snacks, made *of* cheese rather than *for* cheese. And, as the title makes clear, a great favorite of the eponymous Queen.

— Makes about 20 pieces —

3½ oz/100g Parmesan cheese, grated (about 1¼ cups)

7 Tbsp/100g unsalted butter, plus more for greasing

¾ cup/105g all-purpose flour

1 tsp mustard powder

1 Tbsp finely chopped fresh rosemary

Combine all of the ingredients in the bowl of a food processor and process into a paste. Transfer to the counter and knead for 1 minute. Form into a ball, wrap in plastic wrap, and chill in the fridge for 30 minutes.

Preheat the oven to 350°F/175°C.

Unwrap the dough and roll out to a thickness of ¼ inch/6mm. Cut into 2 inch/5cm squares and place on a greased baking sheet.

Bake for 12 to 16 minutes, or until crisp and golden but not too browned.

Cool on a wire rack. They will keep in an airtight container for up to 4 days.

Balmoral Shortbread

This recipe comes from *Royal Chef* by Gabriel Tschumi. "Queen Victoria had a little of this almost every day," writes Tschumi. As did Edward VII. I have adapted it to the modern kitchen, seeing as most of us sadly don't possess vast cast-iron, solid-fuel cookers.

— Makes about 32 pieces —

1 cup/225g unsalted butter, softened

½ cup/100g sugar, plus more for sprinkling

¼ tsp salt

2½ cups/350g all-purpose flour, plus more for dusting

You will need

2-inch/5cm round biscuit cutter

Using a handheld mixer or a stand mixer with the paddle attachment, cream the butter, sugar, and salt together until pale and smooth. Add the flour and work in until smooth and thoroughly combined, but do not overmix or this will toughen the shortbread.

Turn the mixture out onto a lightly floured counter and roll out to a thickness of ⅛ to ¼ inch/3 to 6mm. Cut out rounds using the biscuit cutter, arrange on parchment-lined baking sheets, and prick with a fork. ("Shortbread was always pricked in the same way at Buckingham Palace, in a domino pattern with three rows of three dots," writes Tschumi.)

Sprinkle with a little sugar and chill in the fridge for 20 minutes.

Meanwhile, preheat the oven to 325°F/165°C.

Bake the shortbreads for 15 to 18 minutes, until golden. Allow to cool on a wire rack.

Welsh Teabread

This is a recipe from the kitchen of Charles III. It was served when the King (then Prince of Wales) was in Wales, but it is still popular at tea wherever he may be.

— Serves 8 —

1 mug golden raisins

1 mug raisins or dried currants

¼ mug mixed candied citrus peel, finely chopped

1 mug brown sugar

1 mug strong Earl Grey or smoked black tea, hot

1 egg, beaten

1½ mugs self-rising flour

Butter, for greasing

Combine the dried fruit, citrus peel, and sugar in a large mixing bowl. Pour the tea over the mixture and let soak for a few hours.

Meanwhile, preheat the oven to 300°F/150°C.

Give the fruit mixture a stir and stir in the egg, then fold in the flour to make a soft batter.

Grease and line a 9 by 5-inch loaf pan with parchment paper, then pour in the batter and bake for just more than 1 hour, until an inserted skewer comes out clean.

Turn out onto a wire rack to cool. Serve on its own or slathered with butter. This will keep well in an airtight container for up to 5 days.

Burn O'Vat Rock Cakes

"These rock cakes are named after Burn O'Vat, a beauty spot close to Balmoral between Ballater and Aboyne," writes Michael Sealey in *A Taste of Mey*. "They were served to the Royal Family for teas and picnics in Scotland."

— Makes 8 —

5 Tbsp/75g cold unsalted butter, diced, plus more for greasing

1¾ cups/245g self-rising flour

6 Tbsp/75g demerara sugar, plus more for sprinkling

½ cup/75g mixed dried fruit, such as raisins (golden or brown), currants, dried cherries, or chopped apricots

3 Tbsp mixed chopped candied citrus peel

1 tsp mixed spice (a mixture of allspice, cinnamon, nutmeg, mace, coriander, cloves, ginger, and cardamom, or use pumpkin pie spice)

1 egg, lightly beaten

¼ cup/60ml whole milk, plus more as needed

Preheat the oven to 350°F/175°C; grease a baking sheet.

Combine the flour and sugar in a mixing bowl and use your fingers or a pastry cutter to rub in the butter until the mixture resembles sand. Add the dried fruit, citrus peel, and spice and stir into the sandy mixture. Add the egg and enough milk to bind the mixture to a rough, thick, doughy texture.

Using a spoon, shape the mixture into rough balls, then place on the prepared baking sheet and flatten slightly. Sprinkle with sugar, then bake for 25 to 35 minutes, or until firm and golden brown.

Turn out onto a wire rack to cool. Eat warm or at room temperature, ideally the same day.

Jam Puffs

These were firm favorites at the Queen Mother's hillside picnics at the Castle of Mey. But newcomers beware. There is definitely an art to eating them, and one that wasn't always made clear. As the Earl of Caithness remembers, "I had to eat it in my fingers and firstly bite off a corner before pouring in the cream. I then had to eat it making as little mess as possible. There was a great deal of laughter from everyone else as the cream firstly ran out of my hands and then dripped on to whatever was below. I just hoped that a new guest would arrive soon to complete the challenge!" This recipe comes from Sue Collings, in *A Taste of Mey*.

— Makes 12 to 16 —

All-purpose flour for dusting

One 14- to 16-oz/400 to 457g frozen puff pastry, thawed

⅓ cup/100g jam or marmalade

1 egg, beaten

Confectioners' sugar for dusting

Heavy cream for serving (optional)

You will need

3-inch/7.5cm round biscuit cutter

Dust the work surface with flour and roll out the pastry to a thickness of no more than ¹⁄₁₆ inch/2mm. Chill the pastry for 15 minutes, then stamp out twelve to sixteen rounds with the biscuit cutter.

Spoon a scant 1 tsp of jam in the center of each pastry round. Lightly brush around the jam with beaten egg, then fold the pastry in half to form a half moon. Use finger and thumb to press around the edges to seal, then use a fork to crimp the edges of each parcel. (Do not prick the top as this will let the filling out.)

Place on a parchment-lined baking sheet and chill for 15 minutes. Meanwhile, preheat the oven to 350°F/175°C.

Bake the puffs on the middle rack of the oven until golden brown, 18 to 24 minutes.

Let cool, then lightly dust with confectioners' sugar and serve with cream, if desired.

Food on an Ocean Wave

"The real test of a good chef," noted Gabriel Tschumi, "is whether or not he can prepare a ten-course royal meal on a small paddle steamer in rough weather, sharing the galley with a good many of the crew." As magnificent as the interiors of *Victoria and Albert II* were, all thick Brussels carpet, plush banquettes, and huge open fireplaces, the galley was pretty near hellish. Not only was it minute, and unbearably hot, too, but the five-man brigade had to share their space with the ship's company cooks. "Those slightly frayed tempers which resulted from these encounters made it difficult to concentrate on the preparation of a sauce or the making of a poulet Danoise."

Things were a little better on *Victoria and Albert III*, launched in May 1899. With her vast, steam-powered engines and twin-screw propulsion, two yellow funnels and three towering masts, she was faster, and more comfortable, than her predecessor. She carried a crew of three hundred and a household staff of thirty. And although the galley had rather more space, cooking was done on coal ranges. With limited ventilation. "You only had to turn your back for the wind to change," said Tschumi, "and unless you were very quick a soufflé or a lark pudding was soon ruined in a cold oven." Conversely, when the fires were raging, the galley was as hot as Hades. On one occasion, Edward VII came down to visit. "Phew! I'm glad that's over," he muttered, as he emerged from the inferno, his face beet red and gleaming with sweat. He never ventured down there again.

Edward, of course, expected exactly the same high standards of cooking onboard as he did at any other royal residence, with up to twelve courses at both lunch and dinner. Lamb cutlets, roast grouse, and dressed crabs for the Shah of Iran. Pea soup, baby sea bass, roast beef, and asparagus for a summer lunch just off Venice. In contrast to his father, George V (despite being a fine sailor) liked neither rich food nor rough seas.

Britannia, though, who launched in April 1953, was perhaps the greatest yacht of them all. While the galley was by no means as capacious as the kitchens at Buckingham Palace, it could easily cater for a state banquet for fifty-six in the dining room. Food was prepared by the Buckingham Palace chefs, assisted by head navy cook "Swampy" Marsh, and sent up two floors above via an elevator. Menus would feature a drawing of the ship, just as they had in Victoria and Edward's day. By the reign of Queen Elizabeth II, dinners rarely went beyond three courses. But the sleekly elegant majesty of *Britannia*, as she glided into ports across the world, cannot be underestimated. Not just a floating palace, but the true Sovereign of the Seas.

Ginger Cake

This recipe comes from Jamie Sutherland, who often sends cakes to Birkhall for the King and Queen. His ginger cake is a classic, with a good fiery kick. Stem ginger in syrup is essential for this cake and can be purchased online or in specialty shops. Golden syrup and treacle are both worth seeking out as well (Lyle's is the most common brand) but honey and dark molasses make acceptable substitutes.

— Serves 8 —

11 Tbsp/155g unsalted butter, plus more for greasing

One 9- to 12-oz/280 to 350g jar stem ginger in syrup

2¼ cups/315g all-purpose flour

2 tsp ground ginger

1 tsp ground cinnamon

1 tsp mixed spice (a mixture of allspice, cinnamon, nutmeg, mace, coriander, cloves, ginger, and cardamom, or use pumpkin pie spice)

Pinch of salt

⅔ cup/130g dark muscovado sugar (or packed dark brown sugar)

6 Tbsp/130g golden syrup (or honey)

6 Tbsp/130g black treacle (or molasses)

1 cup/240ml whole milk

1 tsp baking soda

2 eggs, lightly beaten

You will need

High-sided 8-inch/20cm round cake pan

Preheat the oven to 325°F/165°C. Grease the cake pan and line with parchment paper.

Drain the stem ginger, reserving the syrup, and finely chop the ginger. Sift the flour, spices, and salt into a large mixing bowl and use a fork to thoroughly combine.

Add the butter, sugar, golden syrup, treacle, and ⅓ cup/105g of the reserved ginger syrup to a medium saucepan and mix together over low heat until the sugar has dissolved, stirring constantly. Remove from the heat and whisk in the milk, baking soda, and eggs. Using a handheld mixer or large whisk, slowly add the butter mixture to the flour mixture, beating until thoroughly combined. (The batter will be very wet.) Stir in the stem ginger.

Pour the batter into the prepared pan and bake until well risen, deep brown in color, and a wooden skewer inserted into the middle of the cake comes out clean, about 1 hour. Let the cake cool in the pan for 15 minutes, then use a skewer to poke holes all over the top of the cake. Pour any remaining ginger syrup over the top and let sit for 20 minutes. Cover a wire rack with a clean kitchen towel and turn the cake out onto it, then turn the cake right side up and let cool completely.

Wrap the cake in aluminum foil and store in an airtight container for a day or two before cutting.

Two Recipes from
Mildred Dorothy Nicholls

Mildred Dorothy Nicholls entered service at Buckingham Palace as 7th Kitchen Maid in 1908, and left in 1919 as 3rd Kitchen Maid. She left behind a handwritten book of recipes, which is kept in the Royal Archive at Windsor. There's something rather thrilling about primary sources like this; a direct link to the royal kitchens, a glimpse of real history. Her hand is mainly neat (but occasionally illegible), and her recipes precise, although, as is the case with people who cook every day, the recipes can be a little vague. So I've added to and modernized them somewhat. But she gives us a fascinating firsthand insight into royal eating in the early twentieth century.

Swiss Roll

The choice of jam is up to you, but do spread with a generous hand.

— Serves 6 to 8 —

Unsalted butter for greasing

All-purpose flour for dusting

6 eggs

Pinch of salt

1 cup plus 2 Tbsp/225g superfine sugar, plus more for dusting

4½ cups/220g dry white breadcrumbs

⅓ cup/100g good-quality jam

You will need

12 by 16-inch/30 by 40cm Swiss roll pan or high-sided rimmed baking sheet

Preheat the oven to 350°F/175°C. Grease the pan and coat with flour, tapping out any extra, then line the bottom with greased and floured parchment paper.

Separate the eggs, placing the yolks in one large mixing bowl and the whites in another.

Use a whisk to beat the egg whites with a pinch of salt until they hold stiff peaks.

Using a handheld mixer, beat the yolks with the sugar until pale and the mixture holds a ribbon trail when the whisk is lifted from the bowl, about 2 minutes.

Stir the breadcrumbs into the yolk mixture, then fold in one-third of the egg whites to lighten. Gently fold in the remaining egg whites in two batches.

Carefully pour the batter into the prepared pan and spread into an even layer. Bake until set and golden, 15 to 20 minutes.

Carefully flip the cake out of the pan onto a large sheet of parchment paper that has been liberally dusted with sugar. Peel off the top sheet of parchment and spread the sponge evenly with the jam. Trim all four sides of the sponge, then score a line across the sponge about ¾ inch/2cm from one of the short edges (this should make the first roll of the sponge easier to do). With the scored side closest to you, roll the cake away from you into a tight spiral using the sugared paper to support the cake as you go.

Slide onto a serving platter and let cool completely before cutting into slices to serve.

Ginger Nuts

Another recipe taken from royal kitchen maid Mildred Dorothy Nicholls's cookbook. A classic British biscuit, and incredibly easy to make, too. Feel free to up the ginger if you want more bite.

— Makes 12 biscuits —

¾ cup plus 2 Tbsp/120g self-rising flour

2 tsp ground ginger

1 tsp baking soda

¼ cup/50g sugar

¼ cup/55g unsalted butter, at room temperature

3 Tbsp/45g golden syrup (or honey)

Preheat the oven to 350°F/175°C and line a rimmed baking sheet with parchment paper.

Sift the flour, ginger, and baking soda into a bowl, add the sugar, and whisk to combine. Add the butter in small pieces and rub in using your fingers, as if making a crumble topping.

Add the syrup and mix into a big sticky ball, adding water bit by bit, as needed, until the dough comes together. Divide the mixture into twelve pieces and roll into balls in your hands (each ball should be roughly the size of an unshelled walnut). Place on the prepared baking sheet and flatten slightly with the heel of your hand. Leave a decent amount of space between each biscuit to allow for spreading during baking.

Bake until firm and golden, 10 to 12 minutes. Let cool on a wire rack.

Birkhall Scones

These scones are the star at many a teatime in the royal household, crisp on the outside, fluffy within. Best served split in half, with clotted cream and strawberry or raspberry jam made from fruit picked from the garden. As to what goes on first, I don't dare get involved, as the rivalry between Devon (cream first) and Cornwall (jam first) is as eternal as it is fierce. Oh, and it's *scone* like "gone," not *scone* like "cone."

— Makes 8 to 10 —

3 Tbsp/45g unsalted butter, plus more for greasing

1⅔ cups/230g self-rising flour, plus more for dusting

1 Tbsp superfine sugar

⅔ cup/160ml whole milk, plus more for brushing

For serving

Clotted cream

Jam

You will need

2½-inch/6.5cm round biscuit cutter

Preheat the oven to 400°F/200°C and grease a rimmed baking sheet.

Sift the flour into a mixing bowl, then add the butter and rub with your fingertips or a pastry cutter until the mixture looks like fine breadcrumbs. Stir in the sugar, then add the milk (you may not need it all) and mix until a dough comes together. Try not to overwork the dough.

Transfer the dough to a floured counter and roll or pat out to a thickness of 1 to 1¼ inches /2.5 to 3cm. Cut out ten rounds with a floured biscuit cutter, re-rolling the scraps as needed. Place on the prepared baking sheet and brush the tops with milk.

Bake for 15 to 20 minutes, then turn out onto a wire rack to cool slightly (although they are wonderful served warm). They will keep for a day or so in an airtight container but should really be enjoyed as fresh as possible. Serve with clotted cream and jam.

Queen Mary's Birthday Cake

Another recipe from Gabriel Tschumi. "Queen Mary knew that young people liked cakes," he wrote in his book, *Royal Chef,* "so I made a point of providing a choice of three different kinds." This one was served to a young Prince Richard (now Duke of Gloucester) during the 1951 visit that I mentioned at the start of this chapter (see page 101). Among her observations, the Queen had heavily underlined the chocolate cake, and written Prince Richard's name and the words "great success." The famed cake was also served each year at Queen Mary's birthday.

— Serves 8 —

9 Tbsp/130g unsalted butter, melted, plus more for greasing

1½ cups/210g self-rising flour, plus more for dusting

8 egg yolks plus 2 egg whites

1 cup/200g superfine sugar

For the ganache

2½ cups/590ml heavy cream

½ cup/100g superfine sugar

1 lb/450g good-quality bittersweet or semisweet chocolate, finely chopped

You will need

Two 8-inch/20cm round cake pans

Preheat the oven to 350°F/175°C. Grease and flour the cake pans.

Whip the egg yolks and whites with the sugar in a bain marie (a heatproof bowl set over a pan of simmering water—do not let the base of the bowl touch the water) until thick and you reach the ribbon stage (the whisk or beaters when lifted will leave a ribbon trail of batter). Sift in the flour in three batches, gently folding after each addition, then add the butter and fold in until incorporated.

Pour the batter into the prepared pans, spread into an even layer, and bake until an inserted skewer comes out clean, 25 to 30 minutes. Cool the cakes in the pans on a wire rack for 15 minutes, then remove from the pans and let cool completely.

For the ganache, combine the cream, sugar, and chocolate in a heavy saucepan and bring to a boil, then let cool, whisking occasionally, until thick but spreadable, 1 to 2 hours.

Using a serrated knife, halve each cake horizontally and spread each layer generously with ganache, building up to a four-layer sandwich. Coat the entire surface of the cake with the remaining ganache and serve.

Iced Coffee

A garden party stalwart, served in both the royal and main tea tents alike. The key is to use good coffee (this is not the time for instant) and not make it TOO sweet.

— Serves 2 —

1¾ cups/415ml coffee (made using the drip method, French press, or coffee machine), cooled

3 Tbsp whole milk

3 Tbsp heavy cream

2 Tbsp demerara or brown sugar

3 handfuls of ice, plus more for serving

In a blender, combine the coffee, milk, cream, sugar, and ice. Blend until smooth and pour into two glasses over ice.

Lemonade

The other garden party classic, this needs a good tart kick. The perfect refreshment, in blazing sun and soggy downpour alike.

— Makes about 5 cups/1.2L —

8 unwaxed lemons

⅔ cup/130g sugar

Ice

4 cups/950ml sparkling mineral water, chilled

Fresh mint sprigs for serving

Squeeze the lemons into a pitcher, discarding the seeds. Add the sugar and stir until completely dissolved, 2 to 3 minutes.

Add lots of ice, then the sparkling water, and stir for another minute.

Serve immediately with a sprig of mint in each glass.

Dinner

Dinner

Dinner with Queen Victoria could be a fairly fraught affair. Not that one lacked sustenance. Far from it. With up to fourteen courses to battle through, choice was never an issue. But the monarch had little interest in appreciating every last bite, however exquisite. "She eats too much, and almost always a little too fast," griped her uncle, Leopold I of Belgium. The Whig politician Thomas Creevey agreed. "She eats quite as heartily as she laughs," he noted of the young Queen in 1837. "I think I may say she gobbles."

Which would all be well and good. But royal etiquette demanded that as soon as the monarch had laid down her gilded knife and fork the rest of the table had to follow. And even if you were only part way through your *pojarky de volaille*, the plate would be whisked away to be replaced by the next course. Well, towards the end of the Queen's reign, anyway, when service *à la russe* (where courses were served individually one after another) had replaced service *à la française* (where dishes were all placed on the table together for guests to help themselves). Most supping at the royal table accepted this without so much as a mutter. But Lord Hartington, politician and future Duke of Devonshire, was made of sterner stuff. "Here, bring that back," he bellowed to a "scarlet-clad marauder." Silence fell over the room, and all eyes turned towards the sovereign. For once, thankfully, Her Majesty was amused.

After a mighty breakfast and heroic lunch, dinner really was the epicurean (or dyspeptic) summit of the day. It would always start with soup, followed by *poissons*, *entrées*, *relevés* (or "removes," a mixture of roast meat and more elaborate dishes), and *rôtis* (more roast, but usually of smaller birds), then sometimes, as part of a state banquet, another *relevé* course (generally something sweet or a savoury), eventually ending with *entremets* (various vegetables, small savory dishes, and desserts). And the ubiquitous side table of cold joints.

Even on a night at the opera, Edward VII had a ten-course cold feast of lobster salad, various roast beasts and birds, as well as numerous desserts laid out in his private room behind the royal box. All served on gold plates, crisp linen, and scented by vast bunches of flowers. At 9:30pm, the King and his guests would tuck in. Before waddling back in for the second half.

By the reign of George VI, things were rather less extravagant. Second World War rationing put an end to excess (which has been slowly melting away, like one of those sorbets, since the reign of George V), and tastes had changed, too. "It would be naïve to imagine that royalty always dine off rare delicacies," wrote Alma McKee, cook to both Elizabeth II and the Queen Mother. "Now it is only on rare occasions that the Royal family have five courses. Usually, it is not more than three and the food is good but simple." Some gravlax, perhaps (McKee was Swedish), then fish cakes. With brown-bread ice cream for pudding.

State banquets, though, remain one last link to those great feasts of old—formal, ornate, and a gentle reminder of the power of soft, or "soufflé," diplomacy. There may be rather fewer courses these days, but this is entertaining on the most magnificent scale. Presidents and prime ministers, emperors and shahs, kings, queens, and princes. And powerful not so much for what is said (no discussions of policy here), rather for what they represent—continuity, ceremony, stability, and the communal power of the shared table. People brought together by food. Albeit at the most elevated level. No politics or partisanship, no Machiavellian machinations (that's left to the courtiers)—rather, edible statecraft, pure dinnertime diplomacy.

Menus are still written in French and sent up for the sovereign's approval. When Mark Flanagan was cooking for the late Queen he would offer her a choice of five. Highly spiced food is not an option, nor garlic or bivalves. Seasonality is as important as ever, with as many ingredients as possible harvested from the royal estates. "Her Majesty always designed the menus for her guests, rather than herself," he told me. "And added her own suggestions, or remembered that so-and-so really liked this or that the last time they came. Her memory was incredible. All the menus had her hand on them."

State banquets are held up to three times per year, at either St. George's Hall at Windsor (where the table, made in 1846, is 175 feet long and can fit up to 160 guests) or in the ballroom at Buckingham Palace, where a large, horseshoe-shaped table is set up, with the King and the visiting head of state sitting at its center. The whole evening glides and flows like a beautifully choreographed ballet. Flowers bloom, gold glitters, and glasses, six per person, gleam.

The relationship between head chef and palace steward is all-important. Red and green traffic lights are hidden in the balustrades of the far balcony of the Buckingham Palace ballroom. When the lights change, one course is removed and the next brought in. At St. George's Hall, finished dishes are carried out in hot trolleys, most sent up in a small, two-person lift. The rest goes up the stairs with the footmen, scurrying up and down in full livery, "like red-coated ants."

In contrast to all the pomp of a state banquet is a private dinner at home, be it at Clarence House, Windsor, Highgrove, or Birkhall. Soup, an omelette, and a glass of wine. Sometimes, simplicity is the greatest luxury of all.

A Martini Fit for a King

The regal martini is most definitely stirred, not shaken.

— Serves 1 —

Ice

4 ounces/120ml London dry gin

1 capful dry vermouth, such as Martini & Rossi

1 wedge of lime

Fill a cocktail glass with ice and splash in the gin. Add the vermouth, then squeeze in the lime, putting the squeezed fruit into the cocktail. Stir vigorously with a finger and drink.

Les Petits Vol-au-Vents

À LA BÉCHAMEL

Ah, vol-au-vents, the frilly-edged punchline of many a stale gastronomic joke. But this is a dish more sinned against than sinning, a once mighty mouthful brought low by grim, greasy, margarine-infected pastry with a filling that resembles cat vomit. But enough of that. Because a vol-au-vent, well made, is a glorious thing, all buttery, flaky puff, filled with ham, or prawns, or poached chicken, enveloped in the most creamy of béchamel sauces. They pop up on royal menus from Queen Victoria onwards, as both entrée and savoury. And seem to be having their time in the sun once more in some of the more modish of London restaurants. Francatelli has a recipe for *Vol-au-Vent à la Nesle*, which involves calf's brains, sweetbreads, quenelles of fowl, truffles, cocks' combs, and *sauce Allemande*. Sounds divine, but this recipe is a touch more simple. You can, of course, make your own puff pastry, but a good frozen, butter-based ready-made will do the job. And feel free to replace the diced ham with anything else you like. The remains of the previous day's turbot was a particular favorite of Victoria's, although smoked haddock would do just fine.

— Serves 4 as a snack or starter —

4 large vol-au-vent cases (or Bouchées or puff pastry shells), either homemade or bought ready-made, thawed if necessary

1 egg, lightly beaten

3 Tbsp unsalted butter, divided

3 Tbsp all-purpose flour

2½ cups/590ml whole milk

1 tsp English mustard powder

Pinch of cayenne pepper

Salt and freshly ground black pepper

2 oz/55g white button mushrooms, sliced (scant 1 cup)

Two 1-inch/2.5cm slices good-quality ham, diced

Chopped fresh parsley for serving (optional)

Preheat the oven to 350°F/175°C.

Place the vol-au-vent cases on a rimmed baking sheet and brush the tops with the beaten egg. Bake for about 20 minutes, or according to the package instructions.

Melt 2 Tbsp of the butter in a saucepan, then gradually whisk in the flour until smooth. Slowly add the milk, whisking constantly and adding more as the sauce thickens. Simmer for 5 minutes, then add the mustard and cayenne and season with salt and pepper.

In a skillet, cook the mushrooms in the remaining 1 Tbsp of butter until soft, about 5 minutes. Add the ham and heat through, then add to the sauce.

Fill the pastry shells with the mushroom sauce and sprinkle with parsley, if desired. Serve.

Artichokes à la Barigoule

Served to Queen Victoria by her chef, Charles Elmé Francatelli, at Buckingham Palace on October 24, 1841, this is a sun-drenched, Provençal classic. And a regular on palace menus. The name comes, incidentally, from the Provençal word for thyme, *farigoule*, although others claim it refers to the barigoule mushroom, originally used, they say, to stuff it. Small, young artichokes are best, but the bigger ones are easier to get ahold of.

— Serves 4 —

4 large or 12 small whole artichokes

1 bowl of water with the juice of ½ lemon

3 Tbsp olive oil

2 oz/55g smoked thick-cut bacon, cut into matchsticks

1 small onion, sliced

3 garlic cloves, sliced

1 tsp fresh thyme leaves

⅔ cup/160ml dry white wine

⅔ cup/160ml chicken stock

Salt and freshly ground black pepper

For large artichokes, strip off all the leaves until you reach the pale, thin ones that surround the heart. Cut off the stem from about ½ inch/1cm from the bottom of the heart, then remove the rest of the leaves, cutting carefully around the heart to remove any more green bits but careful not to cut into the heart. Use a spoon to scrape out all the fibrous choke. For baby artichokes (with no choke), remove the first two rows of green leaves, then chop off the tips of the remaining leaves and trim the stem. Submerge the trimmed artichokes in the lemon water to prevent browning.

Heat the oil in a heavy pot or Dutch oven and fry the bacon until crisp. Drain the bacon on paper towels and set aside.

Add the onion to the hot oil in the pot and sweat over medium-low heat for about 15 minutes, then add the garlic and thyme and cook for 5 minutes. Increase the heat, add the wine, and cook to burn off the alcohol, about 2 minutes. Add the stock and season with salt and pepper.

Remove the artichokes from the lemon water and add to the pot stem-side down, bring to a simmer, and cover. The big artichokes will take 45 to 60 minutes (use a sharp knife to check if done through), the smaller 30 to 45 minutes. (If the liquid starts to evaporate too quickly, add some boiling water.)

Use a slotted spoon to transfer the artichokes to a warm plate. Strain the sauce through a fine-mesh sieve, discarding the solids, and pour over the artichokes. Sprinkle with the bacon and serve.

Fava Beans à la Crème

Nothing announces the start of summer like fava beans, preferably the size of your pinkie fingernail, blanched, then slathered in butter. When they get a little older, it's best to pop those vividly green kidneys from the tough outer shell. A hassle, but one that is very much worth your while. This recipe is adapted from Francatelli. I've cut down the cooking times, otherwise you'd end up with a green mush, and reduced some of the more extreme Victorian dairy excess.

— Serves 4 as a side —

1 lb/450g fresh, shelled fava beans (popped from skins if too big)

7 Tbsp/100g unsalted butter

Pinch of ground nutmeg

Salt and freshly ground black pepper

6 Tbsp/90ml heavy cream

6 slices smoked bacon, cooked until crisp and crumbled

1 Tbsp chopped fresh parsley

Blanch the beans in boiling water for no more than 30 seconds. Drain.

Heat the butter in a large skillet until foaming, add the beans along with the nutmeg and a pinch each of salt and pepper, and cook for 1 minute. Add the cream and cook for 2 minutes.

Top with the bacon and parsley and serve.

Mushrooms à la Crème

Charles Oliver grew up in the Royal Household under Queen Victoria, left to fight in World War I, was seriously injured at Gallipoli, but recovered and returned to royal service under the then Prince of Wales, briefly Edward VIII. He died in 1965, leaving behind a mass of menus, recipes, and anecdotes. He stipulated that they could only be published after his death. They were, and the book was named *Dinner at Buckingham Palace*. Prince Philip was a very keen cook and Oliver says he traveled everywhere with his "electric, glass-covered frying pan." He also cooked for Queen Elizabeth II, once the servants had been dismissed, usually classic nursery food such as scrambled eggs and smoked haddock, Scotch woodcock, and this mushroom dish.

— Serves 4 as a side —

1 lb/450g mushrooms (wild, crimini, shiitake, button, or a mix)

¼ cup/55g unsalted butter

1 tsp all-purpose flour

Salt and freshly ground black pepper

¾ cup/175ml heavy cream

Squeeze of lemon juice

Croutons or brown toast for serving (see below)

For the croutons

2 slices white bread, crusts removed

3 Tbsp sunflower or other neutral oil

Flaky sea salt for sprinkling

Clean and trim the mushrooms and chop into halves or quarters depending on size.

In a large skillet, heat the butter over medium-high heat until foaming. Add the mushrooms and cook, stirring often, until tender, about 5 minutes.

Sprinkle in the flour, season well with salt and pepper, and stir to combine. Decrease the heat slightly, stir in the cream, and cook until the mushrooms are soft, about 2 minutes. Add the lemon juice and serve either scattered with croutons or on toast.

For the croutons, cut the bread into small cubes. Heat the oil in a skillet over medium heat, add the bread, and fry until crisp and golden brown, stirring almost constantly. Drain on paper towels and sprinkle with salt.

Pictured on page 144

Queen Camilla's Scrambled Eggs

Another favorite growing up. My mother, Queen Camilla, seemed to be able to make huge quantities of these with a minimum of fuss. It was also a Boxing Day staple—some (relatively) light relief, usually made with our own eggs, that always seem to taste better than any other on earth. My father still keeps chickens, which he feeds on scraps, and which scratch about happily all day long. I've never eaten a finer egg. Princess Margaret didn't like the word "scrambled" and insisted on calling them "buttered eggs," which certainly has an appealing burr. The key to this is cooking over a very low heat. My mother does it on top of the Aga range, the pan (which needs to be quite big) half off the coolest burner. Serve on hot buttered brown toast with a few slices of smoked salmon, if the urge takes you.

— Serves 2 —

4 eggs

Sea salt and freshly ground black pepper

2 Tbsp salted butter

Sliced smoked salmon for serving (optional)

2 thick slices brown bread, toasted and buttered

Beat the eggs with some salt and pepper, but not too roughly—just ensure they're well mixed.

Melt the butter in a large skillet until it starts to foam, then add the eggs. Stir with a wooden spoon over very low heat. If the crust on the bottom appears too quickly, remove from the heat. You want thick, creamy curds rather than that awful, overcooked mess with the texture of wall insulator. This will take anywhere from 10 to 20 minutes.

When almost done but still runny, remove from the heat. Put some smoked salmon (if using) on buttered toast and spoon the eggs over the top with some extra black pepper.

Do NOT add a garnish of curly parsley.

Pictured overleaf

Green Omelette

A dish I've eaten at Birkhall and Highgrove many times, this is a take on *Omelette aux Fines Herbes*, with the addition of Gruyère and mushrooms. The key is to keep the outside burnished while the center oozes gently.

— Serves 1 —

5 oz/140g mushrooms (fresh porcini if you can find them), sliced

¼ cup/55g unsalted butter

3 eggs plus 1 yolk

½ tsp English mustard

½ tsp Dijon mustard

Salt and freshly ground black pepper

2 Tbsp chopped fresh flat-leaf parsley

2 Tbsp chopped fresh tarragon

Vegetable oil for the pan

2½ oz/75g Gruyère cheese, grated (heaping ½ cup)

Sauté the mushrooms in the butter until nearly crispy and set aside.

Whisk together the eggs, yolk, and mustards and season with salt and pepper. Stir in the herbs.

Heat a nonstick skillet over medium heat. Once hot, drizzle in a little oil and pour in the egg mixture. Cook, stirring continuously, for 1 minute, then stop stirring and allow the base to set.

Sprinkle the cheese and mushrooms on top of the eggs, then carefully fold the omelette over onto a plate and serve.

Oeufs en Meurette

"The King is partial to an egg in the first course of dinner," remembers food writer Matthew Fort, who kindly provided this recipe. "As I discovered the first time I cooked for him in Romania. This posed a logistical challenge in that the kitchen I had to work in wasn't exactly equipped with the last word in culinary technology. I came up with *Oeufs en Meurette* the second dinner I cooked for him. It's a fine, rollicking Burgundian classic (actually a variation on *Oeufs à la Bourguignonne*) and had the advantage that I could prepare all the elements except poaching the eggs in advance. It seemed to go down quite well."

— Serves 4 —

1½ cups/360ml robust red wine

1 cup/240ml beef or veal stock

1 onion

1 carrot

2 shallots

1 celery rib

2 small garlic cloves, crushed

Bouquet garni of thyme, bay leaf, and parsley tied with kitchen twine

6 black peppercorns

3 Tbsp olive oil, divided

3 oz/85g unsmoked bacon lardons or diced pancetta

1 Tbsp plus 2 tsp unsalted butter, divided

3½ oz/100g white button mushrooms, halved if large

12 pearl onions, peeled

2 tsp all-purpose flour

Salt and freshly ground black pepper

4 eggs

Four ¼-inch/6mm slices baguette

Chopped fresh parsley or chervil for serving

Add the wine and stock to a saucepan. Roughly dice the onion, carrot, shallots, and celery and add to the pan along with the garlic, bouquet garni, and peppercorns. Bring to a boil over medium heat and cook until the liquid has reduced by half, 15 to 20 minutes. Strain into a clean pan through a fine-mesh sieve, pressing the solids with the back of a spoon to extract as much flavor as possible. Set aside, discarding the solids.

Heat 1 Tbsp of the oil in a skillet over medium heat, add the lardons or pancetta, and fry until crisp. Remove from the pan and drain on paper towels.

Melt 1 Tbsp of the butter in the same pan, add the mushrooms, and fry until tender, 2 to 3 minutes. Remove from the pan and set aside.

In the same pan, gently fry the pearl onions until golden and tender, 5 to 10 minutes, shaking the pan every so often so that they color evenly. Set aside.

In a small bowl, mash together the remaining 2 tsp of butter and the flour to form a soft paste.

Bring the wine mixture to a gentle simmer and whisk in the butter-flour mixture a little at a time until the sauce thickens enough to lightly coat the back of a spoon. Add the bacon, mushrooms, and pearl onions and gently reheat the sauce. Season to taste with salt and pepper and keep warm.

Bring a pan of heavily salted water to a boil. Break each egg into a ramekin. When the water is boiling, create a whirlpool with the handle of a wooden spoon. Slide one egg into the whirlpool, decrease the heat to a simmer, and cook until the white is firm but the yolk is still runny, 3 to 4 minutes. Remove the egg with a slotted spoon and place carefully on a double layer of paper towels. Repeat with the remaining eggs.

Heat the remaining 2 Tbsp of oil in a skillet over medium heat. Fry the baguette slices until golden brown on both sides. Drain on paper towels.

Place a slice of fried baguette on each plate, top with a poached egg, and spoon over the sauce. Sprinkle with chopped parsley or chervil for artistic effect and serve immediately.

Oeufs Drumkilbo

They called her Madame Vodka—an accomplished cook running the kitchen at Drumkilbo, a handsome white house in the depths of Perthshire, Scotland. One night, back in the 1950s, some guests arrived late, long after dinner had been cleared away. Lord Elphinstone, whose house it was, asked Madame V to whip up a little midnight snack. So she rootled through larder and icebox and found a few chunks of leftover lobster (this was a grand house, after all), a couple of hard-boiled eggs, a handful of prawns, and some diced tomato. With a dash of anchovy essence for depth, and a few jigs of Tabasco, she mixed this with fresh mayonnaise. A delicious mélange, but our chef did not stop there. She melted aspic into a soupçon of seafood stock, added this to the dish, and topped it off with a thin layer of jelly. Oeufs Drumkilbo was born—a fairly intricate, if enticing, country house curio to be wheeled out at various weddings, balls, and wakes. But Lord Elphinstone happened to be the Queen Mother's nephew. And after one bite Her Majesty was not only amused, but gave the recipe to her own chef. "It was one of my grandmother's favorites," the King told me, after relating this particular tale. And it's still a regular fixture on his menus. A few years back, though, I received an elegant rebuke from one of Lord Elphinstone's descendants, who said that although both the Queen Mother and the King were fans, and the recipe did come from Drumkilbo, the rest of the story wasn't quite true. Which, come to think of it, makes sense, as leaving aspic to set for an hour hardly amounts to a "thrown together" meal. Hey ho. It's still a charming tale. This may seem a daunting dish, what with all that fish stock and gelatin. And it's certainly on the richer side of things. But this is one of the recipes that seems more complex than it actually is. And makes for one hell of a smart starter, too.

— Serves 4 —

½ cup/120ml clear fish stock, cold or room temperature

2¼ tsp unflavored gelatin

1 lb/450g cooked lobster meat

3 oz/85g peeled, cooked shrimp

1 hard-boiled egg, diced

3 Roma tomatoes, peeled, seeded, and diced

½ cup/120g mayonnaise

2 Tbsp ketchup

1 anchovy fillet, minced

Dash of Worcestershire sauce

¼ cup/10g chopped fresh flat-leaf parsley

1 Tbsp chopped fresh chives

Salt and freshly ground black pepper

Chervil leaves for serving

Hot brown toast for serving

In a small saucepan, combine the fish stock with the gelatin and let sit until softened, about 5 minutes.

Meanwhile, chop the lobster and shrimp into small chunks and place in a large bowl. Add the egg and tomatoes.

Heat the stock-gelatin mixture until just simmering. When the gelatin has dissolved, remove from the heat.

In a second bowl, combine the mayonnaise, ketchup, anchovy, Worcestershire, and one-third of the fish stock mixture. Gently fold into the seafood mixture along with the parsley and chives, then season with salt and pepper.

Spoon the seafood mixture into four ramekins or small glass bowls and smooth the tops with the back of a spoon. Chill in the fridge for 1 hour before topping each with the remaining fish stock mixture, then return to the fridge to set completely.

Top with chervil leaves and serve with hot brown toast on the side.

Trout Meunière

A fresh brown trout is one of the greatest of all fish—sweet, subtle, and quietly elegant. But rather difficult to get hold of, unless you're a keen fisherman. Or good friends with a generous one. Prince Philip had his own small loch at Balmoral stocked with both brown and rainbow trout. Although it would have been a brave soul who risked being caught dipping their rod without permission. Rainbow trout, once seen as dull and muddy, is a decent alternative. As long as you get them from a farm where the water is clean, clear, and fast running. ChalkStream in Hampshire is one of my favorites—and is used by the Buckingham Palace kitchens, too.

— Serves 2 —

¼ cup/35g all-purpose flour

Salt and freshly ground black pepper

2 medium trout, gutted

½ cup/115g unsalted butter, divided

Juice of 1 lemon plus 1 lemon, halved, for serving

Handful of flat-leaf parsley, finely chopped

Season the flour with salt and pepper, then roll the fish in the seasoned flour to coat.

Heat ¼ cup/55g of the butter in a skillet over medium heat. When foaming, add the fish. Cook until the skin becomes crisp and golden and the flesh just about clings to the bone, about 4 minutes per side.

Transfer the fish to a warmed plate, then add the remaining ¼ cup/55g of butter to the pan and swirl over high heat until it starts to brown. (Don't let it burn.) Add the lemon juice and parsley, then pour over the fish.

Serve with lemon halves for squeezing.

Impossible Dishes

"Procure a fine, lively fat turtle," starts the recipe for turtle soup, a favorite not just of the royal family (Edward VII always had a thermos of it on hand), but of aristocrats and plutocrats, too. By the start of Elizabeth II's reign, though, it had disappeared from the royal table. With good reason, seeing that around 15,000 turtles (said to taste like a cross between veal and lobster) were shipped live to Britain from the West Indies. Prices were predictably steep, and wild stocks ruinously depleted.

The recipe goes on for pages, including detailed notes on slaughter ("kill the turtle overnight so that it may be left to bleed in a cool place...") and cutting. The soup also required a leg of beef, knuckle of veal, and one old hen. All simmered for six hours before adding Madeira, herbs, and sherry. Even with a large brigade turtle soup took a serious amount of work.

As did many other dishes. "When cuisine Classique was taken for granted no one realised the amount of preparation that might go into one dish," sighed Gabriel Tschumi. *Côtelettes de Bécassines à la Souvaroff*, served at Edward VII's postponed Coronation banquet, involved tiny cutlets of deboned snipe (a small wading bird), spread with foie gras and game forcemeat, then breadcrumbed, put into a pig's caul, grilled, and served with a truffle and Madeira sauce. The King could eat them by the dozen.

Cailles à la Royale was another labor-intensive classic. Deboned quails were simmered in their own stock, the heads removed and reserved, the bodies stuffed with foie gras, then painted with two different glazes, both made from the stock. The heads were reattached using a toothpick, and artificial eyes fashioned from egg white and truffle. Served on a pineapple granita, a good day's worth of work disappeared in a couple of bites.

At Christmas, there was always a boar's head in jelly, stuffed with forcemeat, thin strips of tongue and cheek, bacon, truffles, and pistachios. Then carefully sewn up and braised. Alongside, a huge raised pie in which woodcock went into pheasant, pheasant into chicken, and chicken into turkey. All the birds were boned and surrounded with stuffing, before being entombed in a rich pastry and baked. "When the pie was sliced," remembered Tschumi, "each piece had the different flavours of the birds from which it was made."

And while there is no actual evidence of Queen Victoria eating roasted cygnet (never swans, being tough, with a nasty fishy tang) at Christmas, her son was an enthusiast. The young bird appears on a Sandringham Christmas menu of the 1890s as *Cygne à la Windsor*. And in 1908, *The Times* reported that "at Their Majesties' Christmas dinner one of the special dishes will be roasted cygnets, reared on the Thames, and caught by Mr. Abnett, the King's swan master." Reports of a Boxing Day cygnet curry, though, should be taken with a pinch of salt.

Macaroni au Gratin

One of the very few things Edward VII could not abide was pasta. Tschumi tells the tale of a shooting lunch in November 1903. A well-known Italian diplomat was joining the party and M. Menager, the head chef, suggested that a dish of *Macaroni à l'Italienne* might be included. "King Edward disliked food as starchy as this and made it quite clear he would have none of it himself, but he consented to macaroni being included on the menu when it was pointed out that the Italian visitor might not care for other dishes." This version is rather more modern, and contains—I think—a hell of a lot more cheese. I cannot bear those bland, milky, mountebank versions, which are more white sauce than Cheddar. Here, I mix that great Somerset cheese with Gruyère or Comté for added Alpine heft. Plus some Parmesan on top. I'm sure that exalted Italian gentleman would have approved.

— Serves 6 —

8 oz/225g smoked streaky bacon or pancetta, diced

1 tsp olive oil

3 Tbsp unsalted butter, plus more for greasing

⅓ cup/45g all-purpose flour

2½ cups/590ml whole milk

6 oz/170g good Cheddar, grated (scant 1½ cups)

6 oz/170g Gruyère or Comté cheese, grated (scant 1½ cups)

Salt and freshly ground black pepper

Tabasco sauce for seasoning

8 oz/225g elbow macaroni

2½ oz/75g Parmesan cheese, finely grated

¾ cup/30g fresh white breadcrumbs

Preheat the oven to 400°F/200°C.

Fry the bacon in the oil in a heavy pan over medium heat until crisp. Drain on paper towels and set aside.

Melt the butter in a saucepan over low heat, stir in the flour, and cook gently for 3 to 4 minutes. Slowly add the milk and whisk until smooth, then simmer until thickened, 5 to 10 minutes. Add the Cheddar and Gruyère and stir until melted, then season with pepper and Tabasco.

Meanwhile, cook the pasta in salted boiling water according to the package instructions until al dente. Drain in a colander.

Transfer the macaroni to a well-buttered baking dish, add the bacon, then pour in the sauce and stir to combine. Mix the Parmesan with the breadcrumbs and sprinkle on top. Bake until bubbling, 35 to 40 minutes, then serve.

Fresh Pappardelle

WITH MUSHROOMS

Wild mushrooms are somewhat of an obsession, with Charles III and Queen Camilla deeply competitive about their hauls. In the late summer, porcinis (also known as penny buns or cèpes) are particularly abundant in Scotland, as are the apricot-scented chanterelles, birch bolete, and wood hedgehog. The wild harvest is either cooked fresh, preserved in butter, or dried for use throughout the year.

— Serves 4 —

12 to 16 oz/340 to 450g fresh pappardelle pasta

Salt and freshly ground black pepper

2 Tbsp unsalted butter

A big glug of olive oil

1¼ lb/570g porcini or portobello mushrooms, sliced

1 garlic clove, finely chopped

½ cup/120ml dry white wine

Handful of chopped fresh flat-leaf parsley

Grated parmesan cheese for serving

Cook the pasta in plenty of salted water according to the package instructions.

Meanwhile, heat the butter and oil in a large skillet over high heat. When hot, add the mushrooms and cook until the moisture has evaporated, about 5 minutes. Decrease the heat, add the garlic, and cook for 1 minute. Whack the heat back up and deglaze the pan with the wine. Let it evaporate, then add the parsley and a teaspoonful of the pasta cooking water. Season with salt and pepper.

Drain the pasta and add to the sauce in the pan, mixing well. Serve with Parmesan.

Spring Vegetable Risotto

This was served at Windsor Castle on Sunday, May 7, 2023, just before the Coronation concert. It was the day after the Coronation and everyone was pretty relieved all had gone so smoothly. It was a beautiful, clear, and sultry night, and as dusk fell the castle exploded into light as thousands of drones and flashing bracelets lit up the gloaming. This recipe uses spring vegetables but feel free to substitute mushrooms in autumn or just have it plain.

— Serves 4 —

¼ cup/55g unsalted butter, plus 2 Tbsp cubed and chilled unsalted butter

1 small onion, very finely chopped

1½ cups/300g carnaroli or arborio rice (or vialone nano, although this is more traditionally used for seafood risottos)

¾ cup/175ml dry white wine

4 cups/950ml good chicken stock, kept at a rolling boil

1 oz/30g Parmesan cheese, finely grated, plus more for serving

12 asparagus spears, woody ends removed, steamed for 5 minutes, then chopped in half

2½ cups/325g peas (frozen or fresh), briefly blanched

Sea salt and freshly ground black pepper

Heat the ¼ cup/55g of butter in a large, heavy saucepan over low heat. Add the onion and cook until softened, about 10 minutes, stirring from time to time.

Add the rice and cook, stirring, until white and glistening, about 5 minutes. Add the wine and cook off the alcohol for a couple of minutes.

Add a ladle of hot stock and cook over medium-high heat, stirring almost constantly, until the liquid has been absorbed. Repeat again and again, only adding more stock when the rice has soaked up the last lot. After 20 to 25 minutes the rice should be soft yet firm, with a slight grain of crunch in the middle. Every grain should be separately definable in the mouth, yet surge together as one in the pan.

Remove the pan from the heat and let sit for 1 minute. Throw in the 2 Tbsp of cold butter cubes and beat the hell out of the risotto with a wooden spoon, shaking the pan, until all the butter is incorporated. Add the Parmesan and repeat. Finally, add the asparagus and peas and mix gently. Season with salt and pepper and serve immediately with more Parmesan.

Coronation Food

Even by the sumptuous standards of Edward VII, the Coronation banquet, scheduled for Thursday, June 26, 1902, was to be one of history's most lavish dinners. Indeed, the King announced himself "very pleased indeed" with the menu, created by royal chef Monsieur Menager. The fourteen-course extravaganza would start with *Consommé de Faisan aux Quenelles*, a simple-seeming pheasant soup that took three days of preparation. Not to mention those *Côtelettes de Becassines à la Souvaroff*, minute mouthfuls of foie gras–stuffed snipe, a dish that took the skill of a surgeon and the patience of Job to put together. Not forgetting quails in jelly, and Dover sole fillets, gently poached in Chablis, garnished with oysters, mussels, and prawns. For dessert, gem-like liqueur jellies, and *Caisses de Fraises Miramare*, involving baskets of spun sugar and jellied strawberries folded into a rich vanilla cream. And so work began, in the kitchens of Buckingham Palace, a full two weeks before the big day.

That June was unseasonably hot, turning the kitchens into a sweaty inferno. And normal cooking service, feeding the hundreds of inhabitants of the palace, both royal and below stairs, had to go on as usual—meaning much of the Coronation work was done late into the night. Tempers were as frayed as a dishwasher's rag. As the kitchen staff cursed and toiled, the ingredients flooded in—2,500 plump quails, 300 legs of mutton, 80 chickens, dozens of huge sturgeon, chilled boxes of fresh foie gras from Strasbourg, and pounds of the finest Russian caviar. Jellies, both for the quail and for the desserts, filled every available container. At last, though, on the eve of the Coronation, and after a fortnight's backbreaking work, everything was ready for the big day.

Then, disaster. Menager was informed by Sir Frederick Treves, the King's surgeon, that the monarch was gravely ill. And the Coronation must be postponed. Edward was suffering from an abscess in his abdomen and had to be operated on immediately. The first concern of the kitchen was, of course, their King. But once the shock had abated, another worry remained—what the hell were they going to do with all that food?

The jellies were melted down and stored in empty magnums of champagne, the caviar put on ice, and the quails preserved. But the rest—cooked chicken, partridge, sturgeon, cutlets, fruit, and cream—was quietly delivered to the Little Sisters of the Poor, to be handed out to the destitute of London's East End. The King recuperated, aboard the *Victoria and Albert*, and the Coronation was rearranged for August 9. But quite what the denizens of Whitechapel made of some of the most ornately extravagant food ever prepared is lost, very sadly, in the mists of time.

Pulled & Grilled Turkey

This dish is traditionally served at Sandringham on Boxing Day using leftover turkey and is a particular favorite of the King's. Having tried it, I have to agree. Turkey can be the dreariest of birds, and while a Boxing Day curry can make things rather more exciting, this is a post-Christmas cracker that can be enjoyed the whole year round. It's just as good with chicken or pheasant, too.

— Serves 6 —

1 lb/450g cooked turkey breast

1 lb/450g cooked dark turkey meat (from the thigh and legs)

Mashed potatoes for serving

For the velouté sauce

2 Tbsp unsalted butter

¼ cup/35g all-purpose flour

1⅔ cups/395ml chicken stock

Salt and freshly ground black pepper

6 Tbsp/90ml heavy cream

For the coating

5 Tbsp/70g unsalted butter, softened

¼ cup/35g all-purpose flour

1 egg yolk

1 Tbsp tomato purée

2 Tbsp mango chutney

1 Tbsp Dijon mustard

Dash of Tabasco sauce

Dash of Worcestershire sauce

Salt and freshly ground black pepper

3 cups/120g fresh white breadcrumbs

Slice the turkey breast into bite-size pieces and shred the dark meat into pieces of similar size.

For the velouté sauce, melt the butter in a medium saucepan over medium-low heat. Add the flour and cook, stirring constantly, for about 1 minute. Gradually add the chicken stock, whisking constantly, until the sauce thickens and is smooth. Simmer gently for 5 minutes, stirring occasionally to prevent any lumps from forming. Season well with salt and pepper, then add the cream and remove from the heat.

For the coating, mash together the butter and flour in a bowl until smooth. Add the yolk, tomato purée, chutney, mustard, Tabasco, and Worcestershire. Season with salt and pepper and mix until smooth and thoroughly combined. Coat the dark meat pieces in the spiced butter mixture and roll in the breadcrumbs to coat.

Preheat the broiler to medium and arrange the coated dark meat on an aluminum foil-lined rimmed baking sheet. Broil until crisp, golden brown, and hot through.

Meanwhile, add the turkey breast to the velouté sauce and place the pan over medium heat, stirring gently, until the sauce and meat are piping hot.

Serve the turkey breast in a warmed bowl alongside the dark meat with plenty of mashed potatoes.

Fricassée of Chicken

WITH MORELS & CREAM SAUCE

Another dish served at Windsor Castle before the Coronation concert. It's a classic French recipe, but lightened up for modern tastes. If you can't find morels, use regular mushrooms instead.

— Serves 4 —

7 oz/200g morel mushrooms

1 large organic, free-range chicken

4 Tbsp/60ml light olive oil, divided

3 shallots, sliced

3 sprigs thyme

3 sprigs tarragon

2 bay leaves

1 cup/240ml dry white wine, such as Chablis

2 cups/475ml good chicken stock

⅔ cup/160ml heavy cream

Salt and freshly ground black pepper

2 Tbsp unsalted butter

16 asparagus stalks, trimmed

Steamed basmati rice for serving

Trim the mushrooms, reserving the trimmings, then gently wash to ensure there is no grit inside the cups. Leave to dry on paper towels.

Cut the chicken into eight to ten pieces, depending on preference and size of the chicken (thighs, drumsticks, breasts into two or three pieces each). Cover and chill until ready to cook.

Cut the remaining chicken carcass in half. Heat 2 Tbsp oil in a large saucepan over high heat, add the carcass pieces, and fry until golden brown, turning occasionally to make sure all the little bits of chicken color but don't burn on the bottom of the pan. Add the shallots, mushroom trimmings, thyme, tarragon, and bay leaves and cook for 1 minute or so to soften the shallots.

Add the wine to the pan and stir to deglaze, then decrease the heat and simmer until the wine has reduced by half. Add the stock, bring to a boil, and simmer for about 15 minutes, skimming as you go and allowing the liquid to reduce by about one-third.

Pour the stock through a fine-mesh sieve into a bowl, discarding the solids, and return it to the wiped-out pan. Add the cream, season well with salt and pepper, and return to a very gentle simmer.

Season the chicken pieces with salt and pepper. Heat a large skillet over medium-high heat, add the remaining 2 Tbsp of oil, and gently sear the chicken in batches, getting a light golden brown on the skin side and just searing the uncovered flesh side. Transfer the chicken to the sauce, partially cover, and simmer until the breast meat is cooked through, 15 to 20 minutes, depending on the size of the chicken pieces.

Remove the breast meat from the pan and keep warm while the dark meat finishes cooking for about 10 minutes. Return the breast meat to the pan, cover, remove from the heat, and allow to rest while you cook the mushrooms and asparagus.

Melt the butter in a skillet over medium heat until foaming. Add the mushrooms and sauté until tender.

Meanwhile, blanch the asparagus in salted water until tender, 3 to 5 minutes.

Garnish the fricassée with the asparagus and morels and serve with basmati rice.

Roast Rack of Lamb

The late Queen was known for the simplicity of her tastes, and roast rack of lamb (or *Carré d'Agneau*) is not only simple, but a classic, too. It's certainly not the cheapest of cuts (and do try to avoid that rather tasteless spring lamb). The key is to render all that fat in the initial searing to produce a crisp crust.

— Serves 2 —

2 Tbsp olive oil, divided

Handful of fresh rosemary and thyme leaves, finely chopped

Sea salt and freshly ground black pepper

One 6-bone rack of lamb, French-trimmed

Preheat the oven to 425°F/220°C.

Combine 1 Tbsp of the oil with the herbs and season with salt and pepper. Rub all over the surface of the lamb and let sit for 20 minutes.

Heat the remaining 1 Tbsp of oil in a heavy roasting pan or Dutch oven over high heat and brown the rack all over, starting with the fat side for about 3 minutes, then the bottom side for about 2 minutes. With the fat side up, transfer the pan to the oven and roast for 15 minutes.

Rest for 5 minutes before serving.

Pictured overleaf

Roast Rack of Lamb,
Petits Pois à la Française,
and Pommes Elizabeth
(clockwise from left)

Petits Pois à la Française

You'll find this dish on the early summer menus of all the monarchs, using a mixture of fresh new peas and lettuce. Now, of course, the frozen pea is ubiquitous (and very fine, too), and lettuce is available all year round. It can be served on its own (eaten with a couple of slices of thick toast) or as a vegetable side dish. Without the help of a vast kitchen staff, shelling peas can become rather a bore. I'd far rather eat them raw, with a small pile of salt.

— Serves 4 —

5 Tbsp/70g unsalted butter, divided

1 lb/450g frozen peas, defrosted and drained (or 2½ lb/1.1kg fresh peas, shelled)

12 small shallots, peeled and sliced

1 head romaine lettuce, cored and shredded, but not too finely

Handful of mint, parsley, and/or chervil, roughly torn

¼ cup/60ml dry white wine

Splash of chicken stock or water

Salt

Melt 2½ Tbsp of the butter in a large saucepan, then add the peas, shallots, lettuce, herbs, wine, and stock. Bring to a simmer, then add the remaining 2½ Tbsp of butter, cover, and cook very gently for about 25 minutes, giving the pan an occasional shake.

Season with salt and serve.

Pictured on previous page

Pommes Elizabeth

Pommes Elizabeth is a classical dish from the royal repertoire, which Mark Flanagan's Buckingham Palace chefs "adapted to suit the late Queen." It's a simple potato croquette with cooked spinach in the middle, shaped into a "pear" so "they stand up proudly in the dish when presented." It was served (as it also was at many other dinners both formal and private) alongside the lamb at the state banquet held in honor of President Trump.

— Makes 8 croquettes —

1¾ lb/800g Russet potatoes, peeled and cut into chunks

Sea salt and freshly ground black pepper

3 Tbsp unsalted butter

2 egg yolks

1¼ lb/570g spinach

Olive oil for frying

For the coating

6 Tbsp/50g all-purpose flour

2 eggs, beaten

1 cup/110g fine dried breadcrumbs

Bring a big pot of water to a boil, add the potatoes and a good whack of salt, and simmer until the potaotes are tender, 15 to 20 minutes. Drain, then put through a potato ricer into a bowl. Beat in the butter and yolks and season with salt and pepper, then cover and let cool.

Bring a saucepan half filled with water to a boil (or use a steamer). Add the spinach and cook for about 1 minute, then drain, allow to cool, and squeeze out the excess liquid. Transfer to a bowl and stir in 2 big pinches of salt.

Pat the potato mixture into eight pear shapes, each the size of a baby's fist, pressing a ball of cooked spinach into the center of each one.

Put the flour, eggs, and breadcrumbs into three separate shallow dishes. Dip each croquette into the flour, then the egg, then the breadcrumbs. Place on a tray and chill in the fridge for 30 minutes.

Heat ¼ inch/6mm of oil in a large skillet and cook the croquettes in two batches, turning regularly, until crisp and golden all over. Drain on paper towels and serve hot.

Pictured on previous page

Beef Wellington

The Duke of Wellington, conqueror of Napoleon and inspiration for the rubber boot, was one of Queen Victoria's favorites, "our immortal hero," in her words, both mentor and confidant. An enthusiastic gossip, as he grew older and steadily more deaf he tended to shout rather than whisper tales of various indiscretions, meaning the entire table (usually including the subject of his scurrilous chat) could hear every word. A sharp look from the Queen, though, was all that was needed to shut him up. Famously uninterested in food, one story goes that Beef Wellington was the only dish he would eat. Another claims it was simply a patriotic rebranding, during the Napoleonic Wars, of the French *Filet de Bouef en Croûte*. Whatever the truth, it's a classic of the royal table. This recipe comes from Jamie Shears, executive chef of the Mount St. Restaurant. It opened in 2022 and two of the first guests were the King and Queen. You could also substitute a fillet of venison for the beef.

— Serves 4 —

1¾ lb/800g good-quality, center-cut, dry-aged beef tenderloin, trimmed of excess fat and sinew

Salt and freshly ground black pepper

1 Tbsp olive oil

5 Tbsp/70g unsalted butter, divided

1 to 2 Tbsp English mustard

2 shallots, finely diced

8 oz/225g crimini mushrooms, trimmed and coarsely chopped

Leaves from 2 sprigs of thyme

1 boneless, skinless chicken breast, chopped

6 Tbsp/90ml heavy cream

3 eggs

¼ cup/60ml whole milk

½ cup/70g all-purpose flour, plus more for dusting

2 Tbsp finely chopped fresh parsley

One 14-oz/400g sheet puff pastry, thawed (or two 8- to 9-oz/225 to 255g sheets, overlapped slightly)

Season the beef generously with salt and pepper. Heat the oil and 2 Tbsp of the butter in a large skillet over high heat. When the butter is foaming and the pan is hot, add the beef and sear on all sides until deep golden brown. Remove from the pan and set aside, reserving the pan. Once cool, brush the meat all over with the mustard.

Add the shallots and 2 Tbsp of the butter to the pan and sweat over low heat until soft, about 5 minutes.

Add the mushrooms to the bowl of a food processor and pulse until finely chopped. Transfer the mushrooms to the pan with the shallots, reserving the food processor, then add the thyme and season with salt and pepper. Increase the heat to medium and cook,

continued overleaf

stirring often, until all the moisture has evaporated, about 10 minutes. Transfer the mixture to a bowl and let cool.

Add the chicken to the food processor and blitz until smooth. Add the cream, season with salt and pepper, and pulse until it forms a paste. Add to the bowl with the cooled mushroom mixture and stir to combine, then cover and chill until ready to use.

In a bowl, whisk 2 of the eggs with the milk and flour until smooth. Add the parsley and season with salt and pepper. Beat the remaining egg in a second bowl and set aside.

Melt the remaining 1 Tbsp of butter in an 8-inch/20cm nonstick skillet over medium heat. Pour in a thin layer of the batter then quickly swirl the pan so the batter forms a thin, even layer. Cook until golden on the underside, about 1 minute. Flip the pancake and cook for 30 seconds. Remove from the pan and repeat to make three more pancakes. Let cool.

Lightly dust the counter with flour and roll out the pastry to a 12 by 16-inch/30 by 40cm rectangle. Arrange the pancakes, slightly overlapping, down the length of the pastry, leaving a ¾ inch/2cm border all around. Spread the pancakes with the mushroom mixture and place the seared beef on top. Brush the edges of the pastry with the beaten egg and fold the sides in, then brush with egg again and roll the pastry around the beef in a tight cylinder. Cover tightly with plastic wrap and chill in the fridge for 1 to 4 hours to set. Reserve the remaining egg wash.

When ready to cook, preheat the oven to 400°F/200°C.

Unwrap the Wellington and place on a rimmed baking sheet. Brush the pastry all over with the beaten egg and cook until crisp and golden brown, 45 to 50 minutes. (After 45 minutes the beef will be medium rare; after 50 minutes it will be medium.)

Remove from the oven and let rest for 20 minutes. Slice your Wellington into four thick slices to serve.

Trilogy of Mutton

"The recipe for the Trilogy of Mutton was specially created for the Prince of Wales and the launch of the Mutton Renaissance Campaign," says John Williams, executive chef at The Ritz, and a man who has cooked for the Queen Mother, Queen Elizabeth II, and the King. "His Majesty wanted to show the versatility of mutton, having it served as a trilogy. I felt very honored as the occasion was to popularize mutton, which had gone out of fashion. Ultimately, it was to help the farmers who were losing money on mutton, only receiving very small amounts of money for the fleece. We had to help the farmers get a fair price. The lunch was held in the Ritz Restaurant and there were lots of dignitaries, but without the Prince of Wales, now King Charles III, this would simply not have taken off. But, rest assured, it certainly did with the King behind it!"

Slow Pot Roast Loin

OF MUTTON

Ask the butcher for the mutton bones from prepping the loin, which should be added to the cooking liquid to give extra flavor to the sauce. Serve with roasted mixed vegetables, such as carrots, parsnips, and beets, and creamed potatoes finished with Gruyère cheese and chives.

— Serves 6 —

2 Tbsp light olive oil

2 to 2½ lb/900g to 1.1kg boned and rolled mutton loin (ask the butcher for the bones)

Salt and freshly ground black pepper

1 small onion, diced

1 small carrot, diced

1 small leek, white part only, diced

½ celery rib, diced

5 garlic cloves, peeled

1 bouquet garni (1 sprig each of thyme, parsley, and tarragon and 1 bay leaf tied with kitchen twine)

¾ cup/175ml dry white wine

2 cups/475ml rich brown veal or chicken stock

¼ cup/55g unsalted butter, at room temperature, diced

1 sprig each of tarragon, parsley, and mint, leaves finely chopped

Continued overleaf and pictured on page 180

Preheat the oven to 300°F/150°C. Heat the oil in a heavy pot or Dutch oven over high heat. Season the mutton all over with salt and pepper, then add to the pot and brown well on all sides. Remove the meat and set aside. Add the mutton bones to the pot (if using) and brown these, too.

Add the onion, carrot, leek, celery, and garlic to the pot, decrease the heat to low, and gently sweat the vegetables, stirring often, until softened, about 10 minutes. Add the bouquet garni and wine and cook until the liquid has reduced by half. Add the stock, return to a boil, and place the mutton on top of the vegetables (and bones, if using) so the meat is half submerged in the liquid (add water if needed).

Cover, place in the oven, and cook until the mutton is tender, about 2 hours. Uncover the pot, baste the meat with the cooking liquid, and continue to cook until beautifully glazed, about 20 minutes.

Remove the meat from the pot, cover, and keep warm. Pass the cooking liquid through a fine-mesh sieve into a clean pan, making sure that the garlic cloves are pushed through the sieve to act as a liaison and flavoring for the sauce. Let the sauce sit for 10 minutes to allow the fat to rise to the top. Spoon off and discard the fat, place the pan over low heat, and bring to a simmer. Whisk in the butter to make the sauce glossy and rich. Season to taste and finish with the chopped herbs. Serve the mutton sliced with the sauce poured over.

Mutton Pies

You *can* use lamb here instead, neck or leg, although mutton has rather more flavor.

— Makes 10 pies —

2 Tbsp olive oil

1¼ to 1½ lb/570 to 680g boneless mutton leg, cut into 2-inch/6.5cm pieces

1 shallot, finely chopped

1 small carrot, peeled and finely chopped

½ celery rib, finely chopped

1 garlic clove, crushed

2 tsp tomato purée

1 cup/240ml veal or beef stock

Salt and freshly ground black pepper

1 fresh bay leaf

1 sprig thyme

1 sprig rosemary

6 Tbsp/90ml Madeira wine

Three 8-oz/225 or two 14-oz/400g sheets puff pastry, thawed

All-purpose flour for dusting

1 egg, beaten

You will need

4 inch/10cm round biscuit cutter

4½ inch/11cm round biscuit cutter

Heat the oil in a skillet over high heat and brown the mutton in batches until nicely caramelized. Transfer the browned meat to a Dutch oven, reserving the skillet.

Add the shallot, carrot, and celery to the skillet and cook over low heat until softened, about 10 minutes. Add the garlic and tomato purée and cook for 1 minute. Deglaze the pan with the stock, season with salt and pepper, and bring to a boil, then add to the Dutch oven along with the herbs.

Cover and simmer very gently, stirring from time to time, until the mutton is completely tender and starting to fall apart, 2 to 3 hours. (Alternatively, you can cook the mutton in an oven heated to 300°F/150°C for 3 hours, or until tender, or use a pressure cooker, if you have one.)

Remove and discard the bay leaf and herb sprigs, add the Madeira, and continue to cook over low heat, stirring to break down the strands of meat and reduce the Madeira to almost nothing.

Season to taste with salt and pepper and let cool.

Roll out the pastry on a lightly floured counter to a thickness of ⅟₁₆ inch/2mm and use the cutters to stamp out ten 4-inch/10cm rounds and ten 4½-inch/11cm rounds. Arrange the smaller rounds on a parchment-lined baking sheet. Spoon a good tablespoon of the cooled mutton into the middle of each round, leaving a ½-inch/1.3cm border. Brush the borders with beaten egg and cover with the larger pastry rounds, pressing the edges together to seal. Brush the tops of the pies with beaten egg, decoratively mark with a cocktail stick or the point of a sharp knife, and score a hole in the top of each pie. Chill the pies for 1 hour, or until ready to bake.

Preheat the oven to 350°F/175°F.

Bake the pies until golden brown and crisp, about 25 minutes. Serve.

Slow Pot Roast Loin of Mutton, Mutton Pies, and Welsh Mountain Mutton Stew (clockwise from left)

Welsh Mountain Mutton Stew

Mutton has the most dull and dowdy of reputations, seen as tough, tallowy, and the sort of beast enjoyed only by rotund Dickensian types with scarlet noses and a serious case of gout. Which is a crying shame, as it can be the most majestic of meats, having lived long enough to know a thing or two about flavor. Okay, so the very old brutes can be a little overpowering. But give me a hogget, which is a lamb over one year old, over that dreary, tasteless spring lamb any day. The King is right—mutton really is a magnificent meat and this stew shows exactly why.

— Serves 4 to 6 —

1¼ to 1½ lb/570 to 680g middle neck of mutton (or boneless lamb leg or shoulder), cut into 1½- to 2-inch/4 to 5cm pieces

Salt and freshly ground black pepper

Pinch of superfine sugar

1 Tbsp light olive oil

2 Tbsp unsalted butter

½ onion, diced

1 small carrot, peeled and diced

½ leek, white part only, diced

½ fennel bulb, diced

1 small celery rib, diced

1 garlic clove, crushed

1 Tbsp tomato purée

1 Tbsp all-purpose flour

2 cups/475ml brown chicken or veal stock

3 tomatoes, peeled, seeded, and diced

2 sprigs each of parsley and thyme and 1 bay leaf, tied with kitchen twine

For serving

2 Tbsp unsalted butter

12 small new potatoes, scrubbed

12 baby turnips, trimmed

½ cup/120ml water

12 baby carrots, peeled and trimmed

12 pearl onions, peeled and trimmed

¼ cup/35g shelled and peeled fava beans

Salt and freshly ground black pepper

Pinch of superfine sugar

1 Tbsp chopped fresh chives

1 Tbsp chopped fresh flat-leaf parsley

Preheat the oven to 300°F/150°C.

Season the mutton pieces evenly with salt, pepper, and the sugar. Heat the oil and butter in a heavy pot or Dutch oven over high heat, then brown the mutton in batches until nicely caramelized. (The sugar settles slowly on the bottom of the pan where it turns to caramel and will ultimately give the required color to the sauce.)

Remove the meat from the pot and drain off some of the fat. Add the onion, carrot, leek, fennel, celery, and garlic to the pot and sweat over medium-low heat until the vegetables have softened, 3 to 5 minutes. Add the tomato purée and flour, stir to combine, and cook until caramelized, 1 to 2 minutes.

Slowly whisk in the stock, stirring constantly, until smooth. Add the tomatoes and herb bundle, then return the meat to the pot and bring to a boil. Use a slotted spoon to skim off any foam that forms on the top. Cover, transfer to the oven, and cook until the meat is tender, about 2 hours.

Meanwhile, prepare the vegetables for serving: Heat the butter in a skillet, add the potatoes, turnips, and water, and cook over medium heat until the vegetables are just tender, about 10 minutes. Add the carrots and onions and cook for 5 minutes. Add the beans, season with salt, pepper, and the sugar, and cook until the vegetables are tender and nicely glazed.

Remove the meat from the pot and strain the cooking liquid through a fine-mesh sieve into a bowl. Return the meat and sauce to the pot, add the glazed vegetables, and season to taste with salt and pepper. Scatter with the chives and parsley and serve.

Pictured on page 181

Roast Saddle of Lamb

WITH HERB STUFFING & PORT SAUCE

This was a dish served at the state banquet held in honor of Donald Trump, a man not exactly known for his gilded palate. Still, Mark Flanagan composed a typically elegant menu: steamed halibut with a watercress mousse and chervil sauce, for the starter; dessert was a strawberry sablé with lemon verbena ice cream; while the main course was herb-stuffed saddle of lamb with a port sauce.

— Serves 4 to 6 —

1 saddle of lamb, boned, rolled, and tied by the butcher

A big glug of olive oil for coating

Salt and freshly ground black pepper

For the stuffing

2 onions, finely chopped

4 garlic cloves, finely chopped

2 Tbsp chopped fresh thyme

2 Tbsp chopped fresh rosemary

1 Tbsp chopped fresh parsley

Grated zest and juice of 1 lemon

2 anchovy fillets, finely chopped

1⅓ cups/145g fine dried breadcrumbs

1 egg

Salt and freshly ground black pepper

For the port sauce

¼ cup/55g unsalted butter

2 shallots, finely chopped

2 garlic cloves, finely chopped

1 carrot, peeled and diced

1 celery rib, finely chopped

1 tsp finely chopped fresh rosemary

1 tsp finely chopped fresh thyme

1 cup/240ml good-quality ruby port

1½ cups/360ml beef stock

A lusty shake of Worcestershire sauce

Salt and freshly ground black pepper

Preheat the oven to 425°F/220°C.

For the stuffing, combine all of the ingredients in a bowl and season with salt and pepper.

Open up the saddle of lamb, fill with the stuffing mixture, then roll up tightly and use three pieces of kitchen twine to secure. Rub all over with oil, season with salt and pepper, and place in a roasting pan or rimmed baking sheet. Transfer to the oven and roast for 20 minutes. Decrease the oven temperature to 350°F/175°C and roast for 1 hour.

Let rest for 15 minutes while you make the sauce.

For the sauce, melt the butter in a skillet over medium heat. Once foaming, add the shallots and garlic and cook until soft but not browned, about 10 minutes. Add the carrot, celery, rosemary, and thyme and cook for 6 to 8 minutes.

Increase the heat, add the port, and simmer until the alcohol has cooked off. Add any juices from the resting lamb, then add the stock and Worcestershire and cook until reduced by half. Season with salt and pepper, then strain through a fine-mesh sieve into a gravy boat. Serve alongside the lamb.

Savouries

A course popular in Victorian and Edwardian times, savouries would appear between the main course and dessert. Invariably strong flavored (through salt and spice), and often appearing on toast, they made, according to food writer Ambrose Heath (who devoted a whole tome, *Good Savouries*, to this delectable subject), "an admirable ending to a meal, like some unexpected witticism or amusing epigram at the close of a pleasant conversation. It has the last word, as it were, before we turn to the frivolities of dessert."

Edward VII far preferred savouries to sweet dessert, and you'll find various versions scattered through the royal menus right up until Elizabeth II. According to Charles Oliver, "when the Prince [Philip] is away, and the Queen dines alone at Buckingham Palace, often she will settle for just a savoury—perhaps some flaked haddock in scrambled egg, served with a thin piece of toast."

The following six savouries all make good suppers, too, if an eight-course banquet seems too much of a stretch.

Scotch Woodcock

A classic savoury, found in palaces and gentlemen's clubs alike. The Queen Mother was a particular fan.

— Serves 4 as a savoury —

4 eggs	2 slices bread, crusts removed
Salt and freshly ground black pepper	A smidgin of Gentleman's Relish, to serve (optional)
3 Tbsp unsalted butter, plus more for serving (optional)	8 anchovy fillets

Beat the eggs briefly and season with salt and pepper.

Melt the butter over low heat until foaming. Add the eggs and cook very slowly, stirring constantly. After about 10 minutes they should still be a mixture of set and runny.

Meanwhile, toast the bread and spread with the extra butter or a thin layer of Gentleman's Relish.

Cut the toast into triangles and top each triangle with scrambled egg and two anchovy fillets and serve.

Croque Monsieur

This is not the croque monsieur as we know it, as it omits béchamel sauce.

— Serves 4 as a savoury —

4 slices thin white bread, buttered on one side

4 thin slices Gruyère cheese

2 slices good-quality ham

Freshly ground black pepper

¼ cup/55g unsalted butter

Place 1 slice of bread buttered-side down on a plate or cutting board, add a slice of cheese followed by a slice of ham and a second slice of cheese. Season with pepper and top with another bread slice, buttered-side up. Repeat with the remaining bread, cheese, and ham. Use a 2-inch/5cm round biscuit cutter to stamp 2 rounds out of each sandwich. (Alternatively, fry the sandwiches as is and cut in half before serving.)

Melt the butter in a skillet over medium heat. Cook the sandwiches until crisp, golden, and oozing cheese, about 2 minutes per side.

Beignets au Fromage

Hot, savory, cheesy, doughnuts.

— Serves 6 as a savoury —

1¼ cups/300ml whole milk

½ cup/110g unsalted butter

Pinch of salt

1⅔ cups/230g all-purpose flour

6 eggs

5½ oz/155g Gruyère cheese, grated (about 1⅓ cups)

2 cups/475ml vegetable oil plus more as needed, depending on the size of your pan

Add the milk, butter, and salt to a saucepan and bring to a boil. Remove from the heat and use a wooden spoon to stir in the flour, then return to medium heat and stir until you have a thickish batter.

Remove the pan from the heat and whisk in the eggs, one by one. Add about 1 cup/120g of the Gruyère and stir.

Heat the oil in a large, deep pan until shimmering. Add a spoonful of batter for each beignet and fry, about three to six at a time, until golden brown. Drain on paper towels and serve sprinkled with the remaining Gruyère cheese.

Pictured overleaf

Croque Monsieur,
Scotch Woodcock, and
Beignets au Fromage
(clockwise from top left)

Canapés Ivanhoe

Another savoury classic, and a favorite of Edward VII. Some versions (including the one adored by Elizabeth II) also add scrambled egg. In which case, make the scrambled eggs as on page 147, then add to the haddock and cream mixture and serve atop fried bread.

— Serves 4 as a savoury —

¾ cup/175ml whole milk

2 smoked haddock fillets or Finnan Haddie, skinned

1 Tbsp unsalted butter

3 Tbsp heavy cream

Twist of black pepper

Pinch of cayenne pepper

2 slices white bread, crusts removed, fried in butter until crisp and golden, and cut into rounds

Add the milk to a sauccpan and heat gently, then add the haddock and simmer very gently until heated through, about 5 minutes. Remove the fish with a slotted spoon to drain on paper towels, then break into large flakes. Discard the remaining poaching liquid.

Heat the butter in a separate pan, add the fish, and cook for 1 minute. Add the cream, black pepper, and cayenne and cook until bubbling and heated through. Pile the haddock onto the fried bread and serve.

Sardine Cigarettes

A good cocktail snack, as well as a crisp savoury, these have both salt and a sly chile heat.

— Makes 10 to 12 —

Two 4- to 5-oz/115 to 140g tins good-quality sardines in oil

Squeeze of fresh lemon juice

2 to 4 shakes of Tabasco sauce, depending on desired heat level

Cayenne pepper for seasoning

Salt and freshly ground black pepper

4 sheets phyllo dough, thawed

2 Tbsp unsalted butter, melted

2 cups/475ml vegetable oil

Drain the sardines and remove the backbones, then add to a bowl and mash with a fork. Add the lemon juice and Tabasco and season with cayenne, salt, and black pepper.

Cut the phyllo into strips 4 inches/10cm wide and 6 to 8 inches/15 to 20cm long. Spoon the sardine mixture neatly at the top of each strip, leaving a little gap at the edges. Lightly

brush the pastry with melted butter, then fold in the sides to encase the sardine mixture and roll into a tight cylinder.

Heat the oil in a deep skillet over medium heat until a piece of white bread fizzes, browns quickly, and floats to the surface. Fry the sardine cigarettes in batches of three or four until golden brown and crisp, 1 to 2 minutes. Drain on paper towels and serve very hot.

Smoked Haddock Soufflé

This soufflé was also classed as a savoury. Not just at the end of dinner, but as a light supper for the late Queen, and King Charles III, too. Don't be daunted. It may seem a work of culinary alchemy but it's really very easy to get right. The only proviso is to make sure everyone is ready to eat when it emerges from the oven. A soufflé waits for no one. During my research, though, I stumbled across a story (courtesy of The Greasy Spoon blog) involving that slightly bonkers TV cook, Fanny Cradock, and the Duke of Windsor. Apparently, they dined together in his Paris house in 1956 and she took away his recipe for haddock soufflé. Stranger things, as they say, have happened at sea.

— Serves 4 as a starter —

8 oz/225g smoked haddock or Finnan Haddie, skinned

1¼ cups/300ml whole milk

⅔ cup/160ml heavy cream

¼ cup/55g unsalted butter, plus more for greasing

6 Tbsp/50g all-purpose flour

3½ oz/100g Parmesan cheese, freshly grated

1 tsp dry English mustard powder

Salt and freshly ground black pepper

2 egg yolks plus 8 egg whites

You will need

8-inch/20cm soufflé dish or ovenproof dish with a capacity of 2 qt/1.9L, greased with butter

Gently poach the haddock in the milk and cream at a gentle simmer over medium-low heat for about 10 minutes. Remove the fish from the pan, cool slightly, and flake, removing any bones. Reserve the milk mixture.

Preheat the oven to 400°F/200°C.

Melt the butter in a saucepan over medium heat. Whisk in the flour and cook for 1 minute, stirring constantly. Add one-quarter of the reserved milk mixture and keep stirring over medium heat until smooth. Add another one-quarter of the milk mixture along with half of the cheese and whisk until smooth.

Add the remaining milk mixture and cheese along with the mustard powder and season well with salt and pepper. Mix until the sauce is smooth, then remove from the heat and whisk for about 1 minute to release some of the steam and cool the sauce slightly.

Transfer the sauce to a large mixing bowl, add the haddock and yolks, and mix to combine.

In a second large, clean bowl, whip the egg whites to stiff peaks. Using a large metal spoon (preferably silver but never wooden) fold a good spoonful of the egg whites into

the sauce to lighten the mixture and then fold in the remainder, being careful not to knock out too much air.

Spoon the mixture into the prepared dish and smooth the top with the back of a spoon. Place the dish on a rimmed baking sheet and bake in the lower third of the oven until well risen, golden brown, and with a slight wobble in the middle, about 40 minutes.

Serve *tout de suite*.

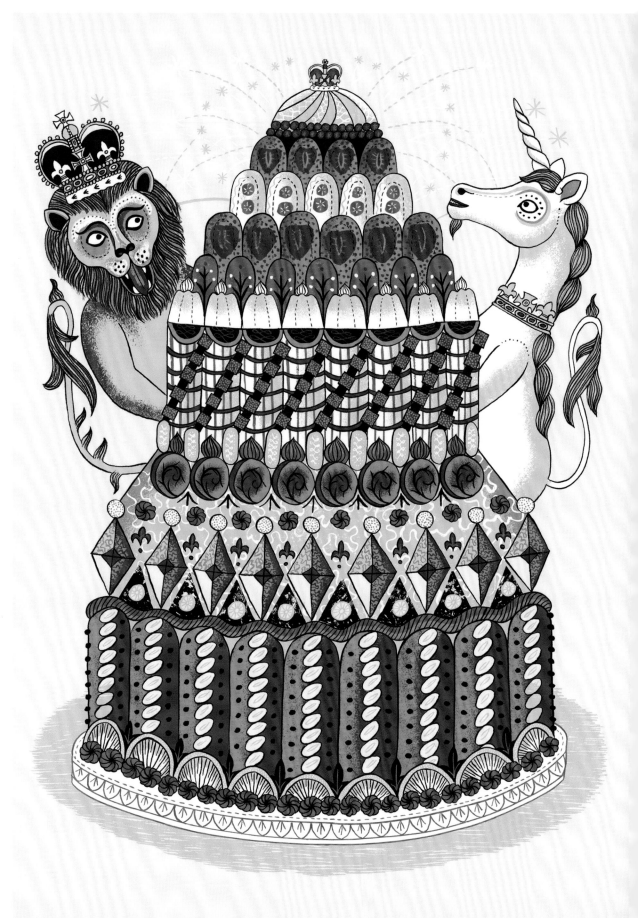

Desserts

Desserts

At their towering, technicolored peak, royal desserts were not so much sweet delights as pure edible architecture, Baroque masterpieces that seduced the eye and wooed the palate. In the days of service *à la française* they would be part of the *entremets* course, served alongside vegetables and other savory dishes, as well as choux buns, *savarin au kirsch*, pineapple cakes, fruit tarts, jellies and creams, nougats, meringues, and spun-sugar baskets.

Ice cream was churned by hand and made in dozens of different flavors, from vanilla and chocolate to cucumber, quince, rose water, and bergamot. It was often shaped into elaborate bombes, made in special round molds, while sorbets, spiked with brandy, rum, and Grand Marnier, were served as palate cleansers between courses. Ice was taken from the ponds and lakes of royal estates, stored in specially built ice houses at Windsor and Osborne, and delivered to London when needed. "Home ice," as it was called, was seen as markedly superior to the industrially frozen stuff bought in London. It lasted longer and was easier to work with.

A quick glance through the cookbook of Charles Elmé Francatelli, who was chief cook to Queen Victoria from 1840 to 1842, shows the most ornate and incredible desserts, towering works of the confectioner's art: Croquant of Oranges, where paper-thin slices of orange flesh were dipped in sugar syrup and then painstakingly attached to a cylindrical croquant mold. Which was stuffed with strawberries and whipped cream flavored with maraschino. Or his *Pommes à la Portugaise*, a *pâté-chaud* case filled with baked apples, apple marmalade, and pastry custard before being topped with meringue. The whole dish, which resembles the bejeweled turban of some fabulously wealthy grand vizier, is decorated with strips of red currant and apple jellies, "which will produce a very pretty effect." Flowers were painted, in colored sugar, all around the base. "None of these were the simple domestic versions of the Mrs Beetons and Eliza Actons of the Victorian world," notes Annie Gray. "Instead, they were moulded, piped, garnished, spiced, shaped, sieved and pounded until the results bore little hint of the raw ingredients, and were elevated into edible art."

Royal kitchens had copper molds in every conceivable shape and size, from tiny darioles for making sweetmeats and biscuits to great towering tubs for jellies and blancmange. The pastry section at both Windsor and Buckingham Palace was separate from the main kitchen, cooler, and rather less frantic. There were waffle irons, pancake pans, and iron sheets for pastry. Everything was made from scratch, including the gelatin, laboriously extracted from calves' feet, taking days to render and clarify. The amount of sugar used was astonishing. In 1844, the kitchen got through more than 2,000 pounds of sugar (bought in fourteen-pound sugar loaves), single, double, and triple refined, as well as candy and Lisbon sugar, which was very fine and had a particularly fine flavor. All that in just one month.

"The Palace bakers, confectioners and pastry cooks … were craftsmen," remembered Gabriel Tschumi, "and some of the finest work I have ever seen was on the sugar baskets for a dessert called Miramare." This dish took three days to prepare and was served at the Coronation of Edward VII. Baskets, measuring six by four inches, were made from sugar paste. "The handle and lid of each basket was in perfect proportion to the base, and the sugar paste was colored to give a grained effect like dark oak." They were filled with vanilla cream and strawberry jelly, with fresh strawberries added at the end.

Queen Victoria was renowned for her sweet tooth, as was Queen Alexandra (unlike her husband, who preferred savouries) and the latter's favorite dessert was her native Danish berry dish, Rødgrød. Her birthday cakes were legendary, too: five tiers of rich fruit cake made using forty eggs and lashings of rum and brandy. At Christmas, 300 pounds of pudding mixture was made containing four gallons of strong ale, a bottle of rum, and a bottle of brandy. All stirred by hand, it was divided into 150 two-pound desserts and given out to all of the staff.

Queen Mary was also known for her love of all things sweet (her husband favored apple charlotte, plum pudding, and pancakes), and always had a huge box of chocolates open on a table in her sitting room. And while the rationing of the two world wars saw sugar in very short supply indeed, desserts continued to play an essential role in any royal meal, private or state, where the Queen Mother and Elizabeth II would mix hearty English classics (Eton mess, treacle tart, fools, bread-and-butter pudding) with French favorites, too (Peach Melba, crème brûlée, fruit compotes, and soufflés). The very essence, in short, of all royal eating.

Fraises à la Chantilly

Strawberries are the very quintessence of British summer and have long been grown in the kitchen gardens of Windsor, Sandringham, and Balmoral. They were (and still are) regular fixtures on all royal menus in the summer, ranging from garden parties to Ascot lunches, afternoon teas, and Derby dinners alike.

— Serves 4 —

8 ladyfingers

1½ lb/675g strawberries, hulled and halved if large, divided

Superfine sugar for sweetening

2 cups/475ml cold heavy cream

Line the bottom of four individual glass dessert bowls with two ladyfingers, trimming to fit. Divide 1 lb/450g of the strawberries among the bowls.

Add the remaining 8 oz/225g of strawberries and a few pinches of sugar to the bowl of a food processor and blitz until smooth, adjusting the sweetness to taste. Pour the purée over the strawberries.

Whip the cream to soft peaks, spoon on top, and serve.

Eton Mess

This classic English dessert is said to have been invented at the eponymous school and served on its speech day on June 4. Although, in the five years I spent there, I never saw any evidence of it. Or tasted so much as a morsel.

— Serves 4 —

2 egg whites
Pinch of salt
⅔ cup/130g superfine sugar

1 lb/450g strawberries, hulled and halved
1 Tbsp confectioners' sugar
2 cups/475ml cold heavy cream

Preheat the oven to 250°F/120°C and line a rimmed baking sheet with parchment paper.

Whip the egg whites with the salt until they form soft peaks. Gradually add the superfine sugar spoonful by spoonful, whisking constantly, until thoroughly combined and the meringue is smooth, glossy, and holds stiff peaks.

Spoon the meringue into eight mounds on the prepared baking sheet and bake for 1 hour. Turn off the oven and leave the meringues inside for at least 2 hours, or until cooled.

Add 8 oz/225g of the strawberries to a blender with the confectioners' sugar and blitz to a purée. Pass through a fine-mesh sieve to remove any seeds and set aside.

In a large bowl, whip the cream until not quite firm. Roughly chop the remaining 8 oz/225g of strawberries and add to the cream. Crumble the meringues into evenly-sized shards, add to the bowl, and gently fold everything together. Add most of the strawberry purée and fold again until rippled through the cream mixture.

Spoon into bowls, drizzle with the remaining purée, and serve at once.

Lemon Meringue Tartlets

We had these at the lunch following the King's Coronation in May 2023. The key is the contrast between tart curd and sweet, billowing meringue topping.

— Makes 4 —

For the curd

Grated zest and juice of 3 unwaxed lemons

¼ cup/55g unsalted butter

6 Tbsp/75g superfine sugar

2 eggs, beaten

You will need

Four 4-inch/10cm tart tins

Pie weights or dried beans

For the tarts and meringue

8 oz/225g shortcrust pastry or pie dough (homemade is best, but good store-bought will do—but ONLY made with butter)

2 egg whites

3 Tbsp superfine sugar

Dribble of white wine vinegar

For the curd, combine the lemon zest and juice, butter, and sugar in a heatproof bowl set over a pan of simmering water. Stir until melted and evenly combined, then whisk in the eggs. Whisk gently until it has a thick, curd-like consistency, about 10 minutes. Pour through a fine-mesh sieve into a bowl. (You can store any extra in the fridge in a clean jar.)

Preheat the oven to 350°F/175°C.

For the tarts, thinly roll out the pastry and use it to line the tart tins, leaving a little extra overhanging the edges. Place the tins on a rimmed baking sheet. Prick the bases with a fork, then line each shell with aluminum foil, fill with pie weights, and bake until lightly browned, 20 to 25 minutes, removing the foil and weights after 15 minutes.

Let cool, then level off the tops of the pastry shells with a knife. Spoon the curd into the shells.

For the meringue, whip the egg whites, sugar, and vinegar to stiff peaks. Dollop generously on top of the curd, then bake until the meringue is browned, 12 to 15 minutes. Serve.

Bananes au Caramel

Alma McKee was cook to both Queen Elizabeth II and the Queen Mother. And this recipe came about one day when she was cooking lunch for the latter at Clarence House. The meat course had gone up when she suddenly realized there was no dessert. Save that is, for a few bananas. "I can remember there was a certain amount of panic about what to do next."

— Serves 4 —

4 bananas, peeled

2 Tbsp superfine sugar

¼ cup/55g unsalted butter, plus more for greasing

½ cup/120ml cold heavy cream

2 Tbsp golden syrup

Cut the bananas in half lengthwise and then crosswise to create 4 quarters. In a bowl, toss the bananas with the sugar to coat.

Melt the butter in a skillet over medium heat. When the butter is foaming, add the bananas, cut side down, and fry gently until they caramelize.

Transfer the bananas into a bowl and cool slightly. Roughly chop the bananas then add the cream, mix well to thicken, and divide among four individual sundae glasses. Chill while you make the caramel.

Grease a rimmed baking sheet with butter. In a small skillet, cook the syrup over medium heat, stirring often with a spatula, until it turns a deep amber color. Pour onto the prepared baking sheet and let cool and harden. Break the caramel into small shards, sprinkle over the banana cream, and serve immediately.

Coupes Montreuil

OR COUPES MALMAISON

A favorite of Queen Mary's, this is little more than vanilla ice cream with peaches. You can make your own, or just buy some good-quality shop stuff. To make *Coupes Malmaison*, replace the peaches with peeled white grapes and top with a little champagne.

— Serves 4 —

2 ripe peaches, pitted and sliced
1 lemon wedge

1 pint/475ml good vanilla ice cream

Divide the peach slices among four individual dessert glasses, allowing about half a peach's worth of slices per person. Sprinkle with a little lemon juice to prevent browning.

Top each serving with two large scoops of ice cream and serve.

Cherry Tart

This is a classic summer tart, adapted from one of Mildred Dorothy Nicholls's recipes (see page 124). Try to buy your cherries direct from the farmer rather than using those buxom but boring supermarket specimens.

— Serves 6 to 8 —

For the pastry

1½ cups/210g all-purpose flour, plus more for dusting

Pinch of salt

½ cup/110g cold unsalted butter, diced

2 Tbsp superfine sugar

1 egg yolk

4 to 6 Tbsp ice water, plus more as needed

1 tsp freshly squeezed lemon juice

For the frangipane

9 Tbsp/125g unsalted butter, at room temperature

⅔ cup/130g superfine sugar

1 tsp vanilla bean paste or vanilla extract

2 eggs, lightly beaten

Finely grated zest of ½ lemon

1 cup/130g ground almonds or almond flour

1 Tbsp all-purpose flour

Pinch of salt

To finish

2 to 4 Tbsp cherry jam

14 oz/400g fresh cherries, stemmed and pitted

¼ cup/25g sliced almonds

Confectioners' sugar for dusting

You will need

8-inch/20cm tart tin with removable base and depth of 1½ inches/4cm

Pie weights or dried beans

For the pastry, add the flour and salt to a bowl, then add the butter and use your fingers or a pastry cutter to rub the butter into the flour until the mixture is the texture of fine sand with only very small flecks of butter remaining. Add the sugar and mix to combine. Add the yolk, water, and lemon juice and mix using a spatula and adding more water as needed to bring the mixture together. Knead lightly to gather the dough into a ball, flatten into a disc, cover, and chill for at least 1 hour.

Liberally dust the counter with flour, roll out the pastry, and carefully transfer it to the tart tin, easing it into the corners until evenly lined. Prick the bottom all over with a fork and freeze for 20 minutes while you preheat the oven to 375°F/190°C.

Line the pastry shell with aluminum foil, fill with pie weights, and bake for 20 to 25 minutes. Remove the foil and weights and bake until the bottom appears dry, 6 to 8 minutes. Decrease the oven temperature to 325°F/165°C.

For the frangipane, cream together the butter, sugar, and vanilla until pale and light. (This is easiest in a stand mixer or using an electric handheld mixer.) Add the eggs one at a time, mixing well after each addition. Add the lemon zest and mix again before adding the ground almonds, flour, and salt. Beat until smooth, cover, and set aside at room temperature until needed.

Spread the base of the cooled tart shell with the jam and scatter with a handful of the cherries. Spoon or pipe the frangipane mixture on top and spread into an even layer. Gently press the remaining cherries on top and sprinkle with the sliced almonds.

Bake until the frangipane is risen, set, and golden brown, 50 to 60 minutes.

Let cool completely and dust with confectioners' sugar before serving.

*

Probationer's Pudding

BREAD & BUTTER PUDDING

This was a recipe submitted to *The Windsor Castle Cookery Book*, in aid of St. George's School, by the then Prince of Wales. The book, put together for the "Children of the Garter," has recipes from the Queen Mother, Princess Alexandra, and the Duchess of Kent and offers no explanation as to why this pudding is for the probationer.

— Serves 4 —

1¼ cups/300ml whole milk

1¼ cups/300ml heavy cream

1 vanilla bean, split lengthwise

6 thick slices white bread, crusts removed

5 Tbsp/70g unsalted butter, softened, plus more for greasing

3 Tbsp marmalade (optional)

¾ cup/105g golden raisins (or regular raisins or chopped prunes)

6 Tbsp/75g packed light brown sugar

6 eggs

Confectioners' sugar for dusting

You will need

8 by 12-inch/20 by 30cm ovenproof baking dish, greased with butter

continued overleaf

In a saucepan, combine the milk, cream, and vanilla bean and bring to a boil over medium heat. Remove from the heat and leave to infuse for 30 minutes.

Meanwhile, generously spread one side of each bread slice with butter and marmalade (if using). Cut each slice into triangular quarters and layer into the prepared baking dish along with the raisins.

In a bowl, whisk together the sugar and eggs, then add the cooled milk mixture and whisk to combine. Strain into a pitcher, discarding the vanilla bean, and pour into the baking dish around and over the bread. Let sit for 10 minutes.

Meanwhile, preheat the oven to 325°F/165°C.

Place the baking dish into a roasting pan and add enough boiling water to reach halfway up the sides of the baking dish, then bake until the custard has set and the top is golden brown, 30 to 40 minutes.

Dust with confectioners' sugar and serve hot or cold.

✷

Gâteau en Surprise

This, according to Tschumi, was one of the Princess Royal's (Princess Mary, later the Countess of Harewood) favorite cakes. One look at the finished product and you could see why. Cake. Hollowed out. Stuffed with ice cream. Covered with chocolate ganache. Hell, it's even got me excited.

— Serves 8 —

For the cake
¼ cup/55g unsalted butter, melted, plus room temperature butter for greasing

1 cup/140g all-purpose flour, plus more for dusting

6 eggs

¾ cup/150g superfine sugar

1 tsp vanilla extract

½ cup/60g ground almonds or almond flour

1 tsp baking powder

Pinch of salt

For the filling
3 large scoops vanilla ice cream

3 large scoops chocolate ice cream

For the ganache
7 oz/200g dark chocolate (60 to 70% cacao), finely chopped

1 cup/240ml heavy cream

To finish
⅔ cup/75g sliced almonds, toasted and roughly chopped

You will need
Three 8-inch/20cm round cake pans

continued overleaf

Preheat the oven to 350°F/175°C. Butter the cake pans and line the bottoms with rounds of buttered parchment paper. Lightly dust the insides of the pans with flour and tap out the excess.

In the bowl of a stand mixer with the paddle attachment, beat the eggs, sugar, and vanilla on high speed until the mixture has tripled in volume, is thick, pale, very light, and will leave a ribbon trail when the beater is lifted from the bowl, 3 to 5 minutes. Sift the flour, ground almonds, baking powder, and salt into the bowl and use a large metal spoon to gently fold into the egg mixture. Pour the butter around the perimeter of the bowl and gently fold in.

Divide the batter evenly between the prepared pans, smooth the tops, and bake until golden, risen, and a skewer inserted into the middle of the cakes comes out clean, about 20 minutes.

Cool the cakes in the pans for 10 minutes, then turn out onto a wire rack and let cool completely.

If the tops of the cakes are domed, slice off the dome using a serrated knife. Place one cake layer back in the bottom of a clean cake pan. Place a second cake layer on a cutting board and using a plate or bowl with a diameter of 6 inches/15cm as a guide cut a circle out of the middle. (Save the middle disc for another use.) Stack the cake ring on top of the first cake layer in the cake pan. Freeze for 30 minutes.

Slightly soften the vanilla ice cream and spread into the hole in the middle of the cake ring. Return to the freezer until the vanilla ice cream is firm, at least 1 hour.

Soften the chocolate ice cream and spread on top of the vanilla. Top with the third cake layer, gently pressing the layers together. Freeze until solid, at least 2 hours.

For the ganache, add the chocolate to a heatproof mixing bowl. Heat the cream until just boiling, pour over the chocolate, and let sit for 2 minutes. Stir until smooth, then let cool for 15 minutes. Whisk the ganache until smooth and thickened to a spreading consistency.

Spread the almonds on a rimmed baking sheet.

Remove the gâteau from the pan and spread the sides with ganache. Roll the sides of the cake in the almonds to coat. Place the gâteau on a serving plate and spread the top with the remaining ganache. Either serve immediately or return to the freezer until ready to do so.

Rhubarb Fool

WITH GINGER BISCUITS & KING'S GINGER

There's nothing silly about this particular fool. It has long graced the regal table, alongside various syllabub and posset cousins, both sweetly satisfying and joyously simple. A great British dish, too, bringing together the joys of the pasture (we may moan about the rain but it does make for the lushest of grass, which, in turn, means the richest of cream) with the fruits of the walled garden. The key is the balance between thrillingly tart rhubarb, sweetened juice, and whipped cream. Oh, and a good glug of King's Ginger (an age-old ginger-flavored English liqueur). Created to "stimulate and revivify" King Edward VII while driving his "horseless carriage," better known as a Daimler.

— Serves 6 —

1¼ lb/570g rhubarb, trimmed and cut into 1½-inch/4cm pieces

¾ cup/150g superfine sugar

Grated zest and juice of 1 orange

2½ cups/590ml cold heavy cream

6 oz/170g ginger cookies

½ cup/120ml King's Ginger liqueur

Preheat the oven to 350°F/175°C.

In an ovenproof baking dish, combine the rhubarb, sugar, and orange zest and juice and toss to coat. Cover with aluminum foil and bake until soft, 30 to 40 minutes, depending on the thickness of the rhubarb. Let cool.

Strain the juice from the rhubarb and reserve. Pick out six pieces of rhubarb for garnish and set aside, then add the remaining rhubarb to the bowl of a food processor and process until nearly smooth.

Whip the cream until it forms soft peaks, not too firm, then fold in the cooled rhubarb purée along with a few dribbles of the reserved juice. Don't mix too manically; there should be some ripples of rhubarb still visible.

Seal the cookies in a ziplock freezer bag and bash with a rolling pin until crushed into small pieces but not so fine as sand. Put a layer of the crushed cookies into six wine glasses and add a a splash of the liqueur. Spoon the whipped cream mixture on top of the crushed cookies and finish with the reserved rhubarb pieces and a drizzle of the cooking juices.

Buckingham Palace Plum Pudding

The original recipe for Buckingham Palace Plum Pudding, found in Tschumi's *Royal Chef*, includes 30 pounds of Lisbon sugar, 40 pounds of raisins, 50 pounds of beef suet, 150 eggs, a bottle of rum, and a bottle of brandy. "Made for the Royal Household at Christmas," the recipe is "sufficient for 150 small puddings, each weighing 2lb." This might be a little excessive for most, so this recipe, direct from the royal kitchen, was shared by the late Queen in 2021 over Instagram. The mix should be made on "Stir-up Sunday," the last Sunday before Advent begins, and left to mature. Times may have changed, but the quality remains the same. If you don't want to use alcohol, you can replace the liquor with orange juice or cold tea.

— Makes two 2-pound puddings —

1¾ cups/245g raisins

1¾ cups/245g dried currants

1⅓ cup/185g golden raisins

1 cup/150g mixed candied citrus peel

8 oz/225g suet or vegetable shortening

2 cups/220g fine dried breadcrumbs

⅔ cup/90g all-purpose flour

2 Tbsp mixed spice (a mixture of allspice, cinnamon, nutmeg, mace, coriander, cloves, ginger, and cardamom, or use pumpkin pie spice)

1 cup/200g demerara sugar

2 eggs

1 cup/240ml beer

¼ cup/60ml dark rum

¼ cup/60ml brandy

¼ cup/55g unsalted butter, melted

Brandy sauce and/or cream for serving

You will need

Two 1 qt/950ml steamed pudding molds (or heatproof metal or ceramic bowls)

In a large bowl, stir together the dried fruit, citrus peel, suet, breadcrumbs, flour, spice, and sugar until combined. Add the eggs, beer, rum, and brandy and mix.

Grease the pudding molds with the butter. Press the cake mix into the molds, cover with a circle of parchment paper, then wrap the tops tightly with aluminum foil. Place each mold in a deep saucepan filled with enough boiling water to reach three-quarters of the way up the sides of the molds. Cover the pans with foil and steam for 6 hours, refilling the water as needed. Remove from the water and set aside to cool completely.

Once cooled, wrap the puddings and store in a cool, dry place until Christmas.

On Christmas Day, reheat your pudding in a double boiler or water bath for 3 to 4 hours. Remove from the molds using an offset spatula, flip out onto a plate, and flambé with a kitchen torch. Serve with brandy sauce and/or cream.

Crème Brûlée

I found this recipe for crème brûlée in a rather wonderful book called *The Royal Blue & Gold Cook Book*, a charity tome written by the Marchioness of Cambridge whose husband, George, was a nephew of Queen Mary. The recipe comes from George VI and Queen Elizabeth and is included along with one for Southern Fried Chicken from Clark Gable. This custard is cooked very slowly in the oven like a crème caramel.

— Serves 4 —

1¼ cups/300ml heavy cream

3 egg yolks

1 Tbsp superfine sugar, plus more as needed

Seeds of 1 vanilla bean

3 Tbsp turbinado sugar

Preheat the oven to 325°F/165°C.

Put the cream in a medium bowl and whisk in the yolks one at a time. Stir in the superfine sugar and vanilla and mix thoroughly but do not let the mixture become frothy. Strain through a fine-meshed sieve into individual custard cups or ramekins.

Bake until the custard is firmly set, about 45 minutes.

Sprinkle the tops with about 2 tsp turbinado sugar each and either glaze under a hot broiler or use a kitchen torch, being careful that the tops do not get too brown.

Chill for several hours before serving.

Gugelhupf

This is one of those cakes claimed by a few different countries—in this case, Austria, Germany, and Switzerland. All have their own take on this classic spiced, fruited, yeasted cake. It featured on the menus of Queen Victoria, who was introduced to it by Prince Albert. At a dinner given by the Queen at Windsor on May 14, 1874, for His Imperial Majesty Tsar Alexander II of Russia, it appeared as *Les Couglauffes aux Raisins, Sauce Abricot*. The dinner had an added frisson in that the young Victoria had taken rather a fancy to the then Grand Duke at a Windsor ball in 1839. "I really am quite in love with the Grand Duke; he is a dear, delightful young man," she sighed in her journal. "The Grand Duke is so very strong, that in running round, you must follow quickly and after that you are whisked round like in a Valse, which is very pleasant . . . I never enjoyed myself more. We were all so merry; I got to bed by a quarter to three but could not sleep till five." The feeling was apparently mutual. But it was not to be. His father, Nicholas I, heard of the nascent romance and summoned his son back home to Russia. He left his dog, Kazbek, as a goodbye present. Lard is traditionally used here and gives a wonderful texture, but I've substituted butter instead.

— Serves 10 —

1 cup/140g golden raisins

2 Tbsp dark rum

1 Tbsp active dry yeast

¾ cup plus 2 Tbsp/200ml whole milk

⅔ cup/130g superfine sugar

2½ cups/350g all-purpose flour

¼ tsp ground cinnamon

1 tsp vanilla extract

Grated zest of 1 lemon

1 big pinch of sea salt

2 eggs plus 1 egg yolk

¾ cup/165g unsalted butter, softened, plus melted butter for greasing

½ cup/70g sliced almonds

Confectioners' sugar for dusting

You will need

Bundt pan or kugelhopf mold

Soak the raisins in the rum for at least 4 hours, preferably overnight.

Put the yeast into the bowl of a stand mixer. Heat the milk until warm, then add to the bowl along with 1 tsp of the superfine sugar. Stir to combine then let sit until bubbly, about 15 minutes.

Add the remaining superfine sugar to the bowl along with the flour, cinnamon, vanilla, lemon zest, and salt. Beat the eggs and yolk to combine and add to the bowl along with the softened butter. With the dough hook attachment, mix, starting slowly, until all is combined, then continue mixing until smooth, 3 to 5 minutes. Cover the bowl with a damp kitchen towel and let rise in a warm spot until doubled in size, 1 to 2 hours.

Meanwhile, put the Bundt pan in the fridge to chill, then brush the interior with melted butter to coat. Scatter the almonds at the bottom of the pan.

Add the rum-soaked raisins to the dough and mix until evenly distributed. Transfer the dough to the prepared pan, pressing down evenly, then cover with a damp kitchen towel and let rise for 1 hour or until the dough has almost reached the top of the pan.

Meanwhile, preheat the oven to 325°F/165°C.

Bake the *gugelhupf* until a skewer inserted into the middle comes out clean, about 45 minutes. Allow to cool for 10 to 15 minutes, then turn out onto a wire rack. Ensure the cake is completely cool before dusting with confectioners' sugar and serving.

Rødgrød

This Danish berry dessert with its deep red hue was a great favorite of Queen Alexandra (formerly Princess Alexandra of Denmark). Although her husband was less than keen—"King Edward preferred savouries and considered *rødgrød* far too sweet to finish off with at supper," recalled Tschumi. It was served with cream and tiny, sweet biscuits made by the confectionery chef. Traditionally, it was thickened with Danish sago flour, but even in 1903 this was near impossible to find outside Denmark. I use cornstarch instead.

— Serves 6 —

2 lb/900g red berries (raspberries, strawberries, red currants, black currants), stemmed or hulled as needed

2 cups/475ml water

¾ cup/150g superfine sugar

1 cup/240ml full-bodied dry red wine, preferably Bordeaux

¼ cup/35g cornstarch dissolved in ½ cup/120ml water

Lightly whipped cream and shortbread biscuits for serving

In a nonreactive saucepan, combine the berries and water and bring to a boil, then simmer gently until the fruit is on the edge of falling apart. Strain through a fine-mesh sieve, making sure you really extract every last drop, and return the juice to the pan.

Add the sugar to the juice and stir gently over medium heat until dissolved.

Add the wine and simmer for a few minutes, then stir in the cornstarch slurry and simmer for at least 1 full minute to activate the cornstarch. Pour into six dessert glasses and refrigerate for 1 hour.

Serve with lashings of whipped cream and some shortbread biscuits.

Bombe Glacée

This was served at the wedding breakfast of Princess Elizabeth and Lieutenant Philip Mountbatten on Thursday, November 2, 1947. As rationing was still very much in force, the menu was relatively restrained. Sole, partridge, then dessert. You can make your own ice cream but it's rather easier to use good store-bought stuff. Just avoid the "soft" versions. You can find chocolate-covered honeycomb candy online or at specialty shops, but you can also omit it and increase the biscuits to 12 oz/350g.

— Serves 6 —

3½ oz/100g chocolate-covered honeycomb candy

8 oz/225g digestive biscuits or speculoos cookies

5 Tbsp/70g unsalted butter, melted

1 Tbsp neutral oil

2 pints/two 500ml tubs good-quality vanilla ice cream

1 pint/one 500ml tub good-quality chocolate ice cream

1¼ cups/300ml raspberry ice cream

You will need

2 qt/1.9L glass mixing bowl

Crumble the honeycomb candy and biscuits into the bowl of a food processor and pulse to create sandy crumbs. Add the butter and pulse until evenly incorporated.

Brush the inside of the bowl with the oil and line with a double thickness of plastic wrap, leaving some excess hanging over the sides. Press the crumb mixture over the inside of the bowl to make a firm shell with an even thickness. Freeze until solid, at least 30 minutes.

Slightly soften 1 pint/one 500ml tub of the of vanilla ice cream, then use a spoon to spread the ice cream into an even, concave layer covering the entire surface of the crumbs. Return the bowl to the freezer until the ice cream is completely frozen, at least 30 minutes. Repeat with all of the chocolate ice cream to make a second layer and freeze for 30 minutes. Use the remaining 1 pint/one 500ml tub of vanilla ice cream to make a third layer and freeze for 30 minutes. Finally, fill the remaining space with raspberry ice cream, cover, and freeze for at least 1 hour or until ready to serve.

Using a knife, trim the crumbs and smooth the top of the bombe so that it will sit level on a serving plate when turned out. To remove the bombe from the bowl, gently ease an offset spatula in between the bowl and the plastic wrap, then invert a serving plate on top and—holding onto both the plate and bowl—turn the bowl upside down onto the plate. Gently pull on the plastic wrap to release the bombe from the bowl. (If the bombe is very stubborn to drop out, dip the bottom of the bowl in a sink of hot water for 10 seconds.) Serve the bombe cut into wedges—perhaps with hot fudge sauce to pour over.

Mango Melba

This is my mother, Queen Camilla's take on *Pêches Melba*.

— Serves 4 —

2 ripe mangoes, peeled, pitted, and thinly sliced

1 pint/500ml good-quality vanilla ice cream

For the sauce

2 Tbsp water

1 tsp cornstarch

½ cup/60g fresh raspberries

1 Tbsp superfine sugar

For serving

½ cup/120ml cold heavy cream, whipped to soft peaks

Blanched almonds, chopped

For the sauce, whisk the water and cornstarch together in a small pan until smooth. Add the raspberries and sugar and cook very gently until the mixture thickens. The resulting sauce can be strained through a fine-mesh sieve, if desired.

Divide the mango among four individual glasses, then cover with the sauce and top with two scoops of ice cream each. Decorate with piped rosettes of whipped cream and chopped almonds and serve.

Royal Kitchens

"I remember on my first days at Windsor thinking how much the kitchen reminded me of a chapel with its high domed ceiling, its feeling of airiness and light, and the gleam of copper at each end of the room." Gabriel Tschumi was writing in 1899, but things have changed little to this day. In fact, it's near impossible not to be moved by the sheer scale of the room. Along with its 750 years of history. Here, in this majestic space, royal chefs from Charles Elmé Francatelli and Messieurs Misson and Menager to Ronald Aubrey and Mark Flanagan have cooked up feasts, banquets, TV suppers, and midnight snacks. "History is everywhere here," says Flanagan. "It's so inspiring to work in such a beautiful place."

Of course, the great fireplaces at each end, both large enough to roast a whole ox, are no longer seething with burning coals. Although those spits remain. And the white walls are still hung with dozens of burnished copper stock pots, pans, and jelly molds, some bearing VR, the insignia of Queen Victoria. A simple clock, above the words G.IV.REX.1838, commemorates the renovations made by George IV. Metal gas ranges have replaced coal fires and there's an extraction system so powerful it whips the words right out of your mouth. All the culinary mod cons are here, and it's still one of the world's great kitchens. A working one, too.

The Buckingham Palace kitchen is rather more modern, but still has more of those copper pots and pans. The old fireplace remains, and the rotisserie, operated by a ingenious system of pulleys and weights. "The iPhone of its day," laughs Flanagan. All is calm here, just as it was in Tschumi's day, where the kitchens had "the discipline of the barracks room." They're a long way removed from the original Buckingham Palace kitchens, built by George IV, where raw sewage seeped through the floor and the putrid, searingly hot air was thick with smoke and choking fumes. Prince Albert not only moved the kitchen in 1851, but made it bigger, cleaner, and better ventilated, too.

Of course, these kitchens don't feed just the royal family, but over 800 people daily, from private secretaries and ladies-in-waiting to valets, pages, dressers, maids, electricians, plumbers, IT staff, policemen, and gardeners who make up the royal household. Under Victoria there was a permanent kitchen staff of forty-five. These days there are twenty-one. Still, the sense of awe remains. "You are sometimes cooking in the same pots as Carême," says Flanagan with a smile. Historical kitchens, then, where the past is ever-present.

Chocolate Bavarois

This recipe comes from Gabriel Tschumi and was served at Queen Victoria's Garden Party on July 11, 1900. I've updated the recipe a little, as the original seemed cloyingly sweet.

— Makes 6 —

3 Tbsp water

2¼ tsp unflavored gelatin

2 cups/475ml whole milk

4 oz/115g good-quality dark chocolate, finely chopped

4 egg yolks

1 cup/200g superfine sugar

1¼ cups/300ml cold heavy cream, plus more for serving

Handful of fresh raspberries or strawberries in summer (or blackberries in autumn) for serving

You will need

Six ½-cup/120ml aluminum pudding molds or small glass bowls

In a small bowl, combine the water and gelatin and let sit until softened, about 5 minutes. Put the pudding molds in the freezer to chill.

Heat the milk in a saucepan until it just starts to simmer, then add the chocolate and stir until thoroughly melted and combined.

In a bowl, whisk the yolks and sugar together, then add to the milk mixture, stirring constantly over low heat until it starts to thicken, about 5 minutes.

Whisk in the gelatin mixture until completely dissolved, then let cool until room temperature.

Whip the cream to soft peaks, then slowly, tablespoon by tablespoon, fold into the cooled chocolate custard.

Divide the chocolate cream evenly among the chilled molds and return to the freezer for 30 minutes.

Pour a pool of cream onto six individual dishes, then unmold the bavarois on top and serve with the fruit on the side.

Pudding au Pain et aux Cerises

Another recipe from Mildred Dorothy Nicholls (see page 124), somewhat adapted for the modern kitchen. The joy is you can use frozen cherries, and thus eat it all year round.

— Serves 6 —

For the puddings

2 Tbsp unsalted butter, softened, plus more for greasing

All-purpose flour for coating

4 cups/160g dry white breadcrumbs

⅔ cup/160ml whole milk

⅓ cup/65g superfine sugar

4 eggs, separated

1 tsp vanilla or lemon extract

Pinch of salt

1½ cups/200g frozen pitted cherries, thawed, halved, and patted dry

For the cherry sauce

1¾ cups/240g frozen pitted cherries, thawed

¼ cup/50g superfine sugar

Juice of ½ lemon

6 Tbsp/90ml water

You will need

Six ⅔-cup/160ml ovenproof pudding molds or ramekins

Preheat the oven to 300°F/150°C.

For the puddings, grease the molds with butter and place a round of greased parchment paper in the bottom of each. Lightly dust the insides of the molds with flour and tap out any excess.

In a bowl, combine the breadcrumbs and milk, mix to combine, and let soak for 15 minutes.

Beat the butter and sugar until smooth. Add the yolks one at a time, mixing well after each addition. Add the vanilla and the breadcrumb mixture and stir to combine.

In a second bowl, whisk the egg whites with the salt until they hold stiff but not dry peaks.

Using a large metal spoon, lightly fold the cherries into the breadcrumb mixture. Fold in a spoonful of the egg whites to lighten the mixture, then carefully fold in the remainder.

Divide the mixture evenly among the prepared molds, filling to within ½ inch/1.3cm of the rim of the mold, then smooth the tops with the back of a spoon. Tightly cover each pudding mold with a square of buttered aluminum foil and place in a roasting pan. Pour enough boiling water into the pan to reach halfway up the sides of the molds and bake

continued overleaf

until risen, golden, and cooked through, about 35 minutes. (A wooden skewer will come out clean when pushed into the middle of the puddings.)

Meanwhile, for the sauce, combine the cherries, sugar, lemon juice, and water in a saucepan, and cook over low heat, stirring often, until the cherries are very soft but still hold their shape and the sauce is syrupy, about 10 minutes.

Let the puddings rest for 5 minutes, then use an offset spatula to carefully turn the puddings out onto serving plates. Serve with the hot cherry sauce.

*

Crêpes au Naturel

A favorite of George V. It's a classic pancake recipe with a little added cream and brandy.

— Makes 8 to 10 —

¾ cup/105g all-purpose flour
Pinch of salt
2 eggs
3 Tbsp heavy cream
1¼ cups/300ml whole milk
Hearty jig of brandy

2 Tbsp unsalted butter, melted
Neutral oil for greasing

For serving
Superfine sugar
2 lemons, quartered

In a large bowl, beat together the flour, salt, eggs, and cream until thoroughly blended. Add the milk, brandy, and butter and stir well. Strain through a fine-mesh sieve then chill in the fridge for 2 to 3 hours. Re-stir the batter before using.

Wipe a medium nonstick skillet or crêpe pan with oiled paper towels and heat well over medium heat. Pour in a small ladleful of batter and quickly swirl the pan so the batter forms a thin, even layer. Cook the crêpe for about 1 minute per side before turning out onto a plate. Roll and serve immediately with sugar and lemon to taste.

Repeat to cook the remaining crêpes.

Bibliography

Anonymous, *The Private Life of the Queen* (D. Appleton and Company, 1896)

Aubrey, Ronald, *A Royal Chef's Notebook* (Gresham Books, 1978)

Bradford, Sarah, *George VI* (Weidenfeld & Nicholson, 1989)

Cambridge, The Marchioness of, *The Royal Blue & Gold Cook Book* (Jupiter Books, 1974)

Cowles, Virginia, *Gay Monarch: The Life and Pleasures of Edward VII* (Harper & Brothers, 1956)

Currah, Ann, *Chef to Queen Victoria: The Recipes of Charles Elmé Francatelli* (William Kimber, 1973)

Escoffier, Auguste, *The Escoffier Cookbook and Guide to the Fine Art of Cookery* (Clarkson Potter, 1969)

Flanagan, Mark and Griffiths, Edward *A Royal Cookbook: Seasonal recipes from Buckingham Palace* (Royal Collection Trust, 2014)

Flanagan, Mark and Cuthbertson, Kathryn, *Royal Teas: Seasonal recipes from Buckingham Palace* (Royal Collection Trust, 2017)

Gore, John, *King George V: A Personal Memoir* (John Murray, 1941)

Gouffe, Jules, *The Royal Cookery Book* (Sampson Low, Son, and Marston, 1869)

Gray, Annie, *The Greedy Queen: Eating with Victoria* (Profile Books, 2017)

Groom, Susanne, *At the King's Table: Royal Dining Through the Ages* (Merrell, 2013)

Haller, Henry, *The White House Family Cookbook* (Random House, 1987)

Hardman, Robert, *Queen of Our Times: The Life of Elizabeth II, 1926–2022* (Macmillan, 2022)

Hibbert, Christopher, *Edward VII: The Last Victorian King* (Griffin, 2007)

Hoey, Brian, *The Royal Yacht Britannia: Inside the Queen's Floating Palace* (Patrick Stephens Limited, 1995)

Jones, Kathryn, *For the Royal Table: Dining at the Palace* (Royal Collection Trust 2008)

Keppel, Sonia, *Edwardian Daughter* (Hamish Hamilton, 1958)

Magnus, Philip, *King Edward the Seventh* (John Murray, 1964)

McKee, Alma, *To Set Before a Queen* (Arlington Books, 1963)

McKee, Alma, *Mrs McKee's Royal Cookery Book* (Arlington Books, 1964)

Murray, Christina, *A Taste of Mey: Recipes and Memories* (Queen Elizabeth Castle of Mey Trust, 2011)

Nicholson, Harold, *King George V* (Constable and Co, 1952)

Oliver, Charles, *Dinner at Buckingham Palace: Secrets & Recipes from the Reign of Queen Victoria to Queen Elizabeth II*, edited and compiled by Paul Fishman and Fiorella Busoni (Metro Books, 2003)

Ponsonby, Sir Frederick, *Recollections of Three Reigns* (Eyre & Spottiswoode, 1951)

Pope-Hennessy, James, *The Quest for Queen Mary*, edited by Hugo Vickers (Hodder & Stoughton, 2018)

Prud'Homme, Alex, *Dinner with the President: Food, Politics, and a History of Breaking Bread at the White House* (Alfred A. Knopf, 2023)

Ridley, Jane, *Bertie: A Life of Edward VII* (Chatto & Windus, 2012)

Ridley, Jane, *George V: Never a Dull Moment* (Chatto & Windus, 2021)

Rose, Kenneth, *King George V* (Weidenfeld & Nicholson, 1983)

Strong, Sir Roy, *Feast: A History of Grand Eating* (Jonathan Cape, 2002)

Tooley, Sarah A. Southall, *The Personal Life of Queen Victoria* (Arcadia Press, 1897)

Tschumi, Gabriel, *Royal Chef: Forty Years with Royal Households* (William Kimber, 1954)

Victoria, HM The Queen, *Leaves from the Journal of Our Life in the Highlands* (Smith, Elder and Company, 1868)

Windsor Castle Parents of Choristers of St. George's Chapel, *The Windsor Castle Cookery Book: Entertaining With the Children of the Garter* (Nicole Crossley-Holland, 1996)

Windsor, The Duke of, *A King's Story: The Memoirs of HRH The Duke of Windsor KG* (Cassell & Co, 1951)

Ziegler, Philip, *King Edward VIII: The Official Biography* (Collins, 1990)

Suppliers

Here is a selection of some of my favorite suppliers in the UK.

Meat

H G Walter
www.hgwalter.com
One of Britain's best butchers, and one of my favorites, too.

The Ethical Butcher
www.ethicalbutcher.co.uk
Excellent quality British meat, bred on farms that embrace regenerative agriculture.

Turner and George
www.turnerandgeorge.co.uk
These men really know their meat, supplied by small, independent farmers, with their beef dry-aged on site.

Hannan Meats
www.hannanmeats.com
Peter Hannan's salt-aged Glenarm beef is some of the best I've ever tasted.

Fish

Wright Brothers
www.thewrightbrothers.co.uk
A huge selection of top-quality oysters, shellfish, and fish. Sustainably sourced, and delivered across the UK.

Rockfish
www.therockfish.co.uk
Not only does Mitch Tonks sell the very freshest fish, sustainably fished from Brixham every weekday morning, he also does some incredible English tinned fish.

ChalkStream
www.chalkstreamfoods.co.uk
Farmed rainbow trout that tastes pure and clean, thanks to slow growth in gin-clear Hampshire chalk stream water.

Flour

Shipton Mill
www.shipton-mill.com
You'll find every kind of organic stone-ground flour here, as well as yeasts and olive oils.

Farmshops

Farmshop
Based in Bruton, this specializes in beef, pork, and lamb from their Somerset farm, as well as some cracking West country cheese and charcuterie.

Highgrove
www.highgrovegardens.com
Organic food from the King's Gloucestershire estate, you'll find everything from jams and biscuits to sweets, mustards, and chutneys.

Windsor Castle Farm Shop
www.windsorfarmshop.co.uk
Slow reared, traditional breed beef, pork, and lamb from the Royal Estates, and some good cheese and dairy, too.

Sandringham
www.sandringhamestate.co.uk
Beer, honey, chocolate, tea and toffee, along with a good range of sweets and biscuits.

Daylesford
www.daylesford.com
Carole Bamford was a sustainable farm shop pioneer, and Daylesford gets better by the year. All the organic meat comes from the Bamfords' estates, while fruit and vegetables come from their market garden. Their cheeses are sublime (don't miss the Double Gloucester), along with pretty much everything else.

Smoked Fish

Brown and Forrest
www.brownandforrest.co.uk
A really great Somerset smokery, who source the best fish, cheese, and meat from trusted local suppliers and work wonders over their brick kiln.

Severn and Wye
www.severnandwye.co.uk
If you are going to eat smoked salmon, then theirs is one of the very best. I love their whole smoked eels, too.

Secret Smokehouse
www.secretsmokehouse.co.uk
PGA certified "London" cure salmon smokers (they also do a fine smoked trout and mackerel). They supply the likes of The Ritz, Wilton's, The Fat Duck, Core, and Claude Bosi. They are also pioneers of "land-based" farmed salmon (i.e. which doesn't pollute the coastal waters), which for me, could be the future.

Caviar

King's Fine Foods
www.kingsfinefood.co.uk
Few people know as much about caviar as Laura King, the "queen of caviar." The only place to buy the best farmed caviar in the world.

Salt

Maldon
www.maldonsalt.com
Wonderful texture and good, clean flavor.

Halen Môn
www.halenmon.com
Another salt classic, crunchy yet soft enough to crush between the fingers.

Ironware

Netherton Foundry
www.netherton-foundry.co.uk
Traditional cast and spun iron cookware, handmade in Shropshire. I have two frying pans from them, and use them every day. They last a lifetime and never let you down.

Cheesemongers

The Courtyard Diary
www.thecourtyarddairy.co.uk
A brilliant Yorkshire cheesemonger that has been utterly vital in supporting artisan cheese producers. Legends, in every way.

La Fromagerie
www.lafromagerie.co.uk
One of the originals, and still one of the best, Patricia Michelson's three shops are London classics. They have a huge range of continental cheese, perfectly kept, but an equally impressive collection of British beauties, too.

The Fine Cheese Co
www.finecheese.co.uk
A Bath institution. Great selection of British (and European) cheeses. And they keep them beautifully, too.

Neal's Yard Dairy
www.nealsyarddairy.co.uk
Another London legend, and pioneers of supporting great British cheeses, too.

Index

About the Author

Tom Parker Bowles has been an award-winning food writer for more than twenty years, is the author of eight books on food (including the bestselling Fortnum & Mason cookbooks), and is the restaurant critic for *The Mail on Sunday*. He is also a contributing editor for *Esquire*, *Country Life*, and *Condé Nast Traveller*, plus a regular judge on the BBC's *Masterchef*. Tom is a godson of King Charles III, and his mother, Camilla, is Queen.

 @tomparkerbowles

✷

About the Photographer

Born in London, award-winning food and drink photographer John Carey has worked on books with Gordon Ramsay, the Ritz, and Claridge's, amongst many others. John's eye for detail and passion for photography, food, and drink mean he has a broad client base that includes some of the most prestigious chefs, restaurants, hotels, book publishers, and brands in the world.

@johncareyphoto

✷

About the Illustrator

Alice Pattullo is an illustrator originally from Newcastle upon Tyne who lives and works in East London. Alice works on commissioned illustrations for a wide variety of clients as well as producing limited edition screen prints, which she exhibits and sells in the UK.

@alicepattullo

Acknowledgments

This book, as ever, is a group effort, and would not have been possible without such an incredible bunch of talented people. I just scrawl the words. The real magic comes from elsewhere.

I'd like to thank TM the King and Queen Camilla for all of their help, guidance, and inspiration.

Stephanie Jackson at Octopus, my brilliant publisher, at long last we have been able to work together. It's been a joy. Pauline Bache, who has watched over, organized, edited, and arranged every part of this book. And Creative Director Jonathan Christie, who shaped its look and feel. Thanks to Chloë Johnson-Hill and her marketing and PR team; Marianne Laidlaw, Veronique de Sutter, and their colleagues in sales for the UK and worldwide; Peter Hunt in production and all at Octopus who have contributed along the way.

To John Carey, photographer, Cure fanatic, and an industry great. Who knew a photo shoot could actually be fun? Huge thanks also to Annie Rigg, chef and author (but definitely not a "home economist"), who cooked, tested most of the recipes in the book, and offered essential advice and guidance throughout along with Hattie Baker. And to Tamsin Weston for the brilliant props.

And of course, Alice Pattullo, the illustrator, for all her beautiful drawings.

A massive thank you to Mark Flanagan, Royal Chef, who went out of his way to help, despite being in the middle of about ten different menus every day; his insight was crucial, his knowledge immense. And Stuart Major, Head Chef at Clarence House, for all of his recipes, too.

Thanks also to Bill Stockting and Julie Crocker and everyone at the Royal Archive in Windsor.

Cleyenne Lazarotto-Miotto, for her endless support, and for reading countless early drafts. And being refreshingly direct.

Hugo Vickers, for advice and quite a few recipes.

Tobyn Andreae, for all of his help.

Matthew Fort, Jeremy Lee, Jamie Sutherland, Tom Pemberton, John Williams, Gavin Rankin, and Mark Hix for their recipes.

Originally published in the United Kingdom by Aster, an imprint of Octopus
Publishing Group Ltd.

Individual recipe credits: page 41 © Tom Pemberton 2024; page 47 © Bellamy's 2024; pages 61,
65, 114, 129, 163, 168, 200, 205 © HM Charles III 2024 and reproduced with the kind permission
of HM Charles III; pages 74 and 184 © Mark Flanagan 2024; page 81 © Mark Hix 2024; page 84 ©
Mark Flanagan 2024 and reproduced with kind permission of the Royal Collection Trust; page 86
© Jeremy Lee 2024 and reproduced with kind permission of 4th Estate; page 107 from The
Constance Spry Cookery Book, reproduced with kind permission of the publisher, Grub Street,
London; pages 117 and 118 reproduced with kind permission of Queen Elizabeth Castle of May
Trust; page 146 reproduced with kind permission of Bonnier Books; page 150 © Matthew Forte
2024; page 174 © Jamie Shears 2024; pages 177–82 © John Williams 2024.

Typeface: Klim Type Foundry's Heldane

Library of Congress Cataloging-in-Publication Data is on file with the publisher.

Hardcover ISBN: 978-0-593-83555-5
eBook ISBN: 978-0-593-83556-2

Printed in China

Editor: Cristina Garces | Production editor: Ashley Pierce
Design manager: Emma Campion | Production designer: Mari Gill
Production manager: Jane Chinn
Americanizer: Rebeccah Marsters | Copyeditor: Rachel Holzman | Proofreader: Sasha Tropp

10 9 8 7 6 5 4 3 2 1

First U.S. Edition